MIRACLES

ARE WHAT YOU

MAKE OF THEM

RABBI CORINNE COPNICK

Rabbi Corinne Copnick

ISBN: 979-8-218-25409-4
Print Publication Date: Sept, 2023
ISBN: 979-8-218-23730-1
Digital Publication Date: Sept, 2023

The author is available for speaking and media engagements.
Contact information:
rabbi@rabbicorinne.com
www.rabbicorinne.com
Mobile: 818.430.3245

8959 White Oak Avenue,
Sherwood Forest, California
91325
U.S.A.

Edited by Janet Spiegel

Scriptural English translations from the Hebrew made available digitally courtesy of *https://www.Sefaria.org* from the Jewish Publication Society, ed., *JPS HEBREW-ENGLISH TANAKH: The Holy Scriptures: The New JPS Translation According to the Traditional Hebrew Text* (Philadelphia: The Jewish Publication Society, 1985).

This is a work of creative non-fiction. Some names and identifying details have been changed to protect the privacy of the people involved. Some of my stories, essays, or poems included in this collection have been individually posted previously on my website (www.rabbicorinne.com) under the category *"Miracles Are What You Make of Them,"* the theme of this book. Others have appeared in various publications over time and are attributed in the Notes. Some material was originally written for my academic AJRCA rabbinic thesis, "The Staying Power of Hope in the

Aggadic Narratives of the Talmud," 2014. Two short selections previously appeared in my article, "Interpersonal Ethics: Our Partners in Digital Citizenship," published by Ben Yehuda Press, 2023, and are fully attributed in the Notes. All rights reserved.

Brief ("fair use") quotes from contemporary rabbis and other great thinkers are included in *Miracles Are What You Make of Them* with Rabbi Copnick's appreciation and gratitude. Individual attributions are all documented in the Notes to this book. While most sources are still available, some links may no longer be available on their respective websites.

MIRACLES ARE WHAT YOU MAKE OF THEM

RABBI CORINNE COPNICK

Edited by Janet Spiegel

DEDICATION [1]

For my grandchildren's generation and their children after them...

Inlay your two hands
directly on my single soul,
impress your mystic caress
right through the transparent
veil that keeps me from you.

Hand-clasp my pen-in-hand
prayer that this poem, yours
for the asking, transmits mutely
the cadence of a mindful Creator.

Rabbi Corinne Copnick

Table of Contents

FOREWORD

by Dr. Joel Gereboff

Professor of Bible and Jewish History,

Academy for Jewish Religion California (AJRCA)

Rabbi Corinne Copnick's *Miracles are What You Make of Them* combines the content and goals of a traditional Jewish "Ethical Will" with the moving style of a gifted and seasoned writer. Like classical ethical wills, Copnick's book conveys to her contemporary family, friends, students, and disciples, wisdom discerned over a blessed long life. This wisdom draws upon personal experiences and the wisdom of the Torah, classical rabbinic texts, the views of a diverse range of contemporary rabbis, and teachers of Torah. It seeks to provide guidance and an optimistic, hopeful message to motivate its readers, especially her grandchildren and great-grandchildren-to-be that encourages them to see the opportunities available to find meaning in daily lives. Copnick expresses her insights in crisp beautifully written prose, artistically crafted short vignettes, anecdotes, and lyrical poetry.

Shortly after moving from Canada to Los Angeles—having already raised a family, served in leadership roles, and written a number of works before her seventieth year of life—Copnick in her early seventies embodied the core message of this book—always to

Rabbi Corinne Copnick

keep on learning, growing, teaching, sharing, and impacting. She enrolled in rabbinic school, learned Hebrew in order to decipher Jewish texts, and achieved the knowledge to share her learning with others, including classmates and teachers during the course of her studies. Over the course of the decade since being ordained, Copnick has shared her learning with many others, including having become proficient in technologically advanced forms of communication. But it is clear from this book, that she has the gift of a well-honed author, and powerfully uses the written word to encourage others to not miss the daily opportunities to shape their circumstances as miracles, as moments for connecting to one another, and to the spiritual energy and forces that pervade the world.

Copnick imparts the motivation and message of her book by recounting a moment while driving in Los Angeles. She relates:

> Suddenly I spotted a beautiful piece of lace, an antique lace fragment lying on the floor of my car. Dotted with opalescent sequins that resembled the embroidered lace decorating my long-ago wedding dress, it sparkled in the rays of sunshine that beamed through the car windows. When, at the next corner, I looked again, a coral-colored silk lining, barely showing itself where the corner of the antique lace

turned back, pulsated like a beating heart. To me, it was not just a relic of the past; it seemed alive. My own heart was pounding, I stopped the car at the first opportunity and reached for the lovely fragment, but then, like a mirage, it disappeared. My thoughts were playing tricks on me. "That mirage is a representation of hope," I thought, "a glimpse of hope, ephemeral, combining past memories and future joys."

Opportunities for making connections between the past, present, and future; between ourselves and others, people around the world, and the divine, are in our hands every day. This book will inspire you to transform those moments into miracles—if we have hope and take action, they will come to be.

INTRODUCTION

*W*hy do writers write?[2] I often think it's because they can't NOT write, probably true as well for those who endeavor in other artistic fields. There are, of course, those who write, or pick up a paintbrush, or have a compulsion to step on a stage, for self-expression or for applause, but I write, like many others, from a burning need to set down my thoughts before they are lost. It's a desire to give them to other people, to share...because, like most gifts, what is written cannot really be given until it is received. At times in my life—which now spans more than eight decades (getting close to nine)—writing has also been a search, an attempt, almost unknowingly, to reach out to the divine, or at least to expand the glimpse of divinity within ourselves as created beings.

And sometimes this desire waxes and wanes...but it always comes back, often with redoubled force. In my first book, *Embrace: A Love Story in Poetry*, a bilingual book which I wrote in Montreal, Quebec (where I was born and lived most of my life) in 1981 as Corinne Copnick Spiegel, I reached out for I-knew-not-what, something inarticulate I sensed was already there. This book "happened" long before I became a rabbi, long before I recognized that there was a compelling path I needed to follow. And I wrote *Embrace* (*Etreinte: Un poeme d'amour* is the full title in French) long

1

before we had the Internet or Social Media or Zoom or other ways—aside from the telephone or telegram, or even the long-lost art of the hand-written letter—to reach out to those, known or unknown, who were not physically sharing our space. *Embrace* is about that kind of spiritual reaching, with its concomitant deep anger and grief about its unattainability and therefore loss, but eventual hope and resolution for the future.

Nevertheless, as I wrote it then, even I didn't realize what it was fully about until much later in life. I was long married by then, the mother of four wonderful children, and with my own satisfying achievements in artistic and educational fields. I knew that the searching had to do with something that *wasn't* there in my life—an awareness that affected many women of my generation after Betty Freidan, Germaine Greer, Gloria Steinem, and abundant other feminists had their very vocal say, for better or worse, in the 1960s, 70s, and 80s. Maybe there's always something that isn't there in everyone's life. Maybe we just don't identify it correctly. Maybe societal changes always create personal challenges.

At any rate, the response to my metaphorical book, published in a limited edition (because, if they don't know you, who buys poetry?) was very positive, and the book sold out. I was gratified to be invited to join the prestigious writers' group, PEN Canada, at a time in Quebec when the organization included both English-language and French-language writers. Today my bilingual

Embrace/Etreinte is considered a rare book. Whenever I can find a used one in an online bookstore, I purchase it (if the price is at all affordable) for myself.

My next book of stories and poems, *Altar Pieces,* continued the theme of striving to come ever closer to the divine, this time in mystical longing expressed in ritual. Together with two of my daughters, Janet and Shelley Spiegel, we filmed the stories, which were illustrated by the Canadian artist, Saul Field, renowned for his etchings. As an experienced actress, I served as narrator of the stories, along with my talented daughters—Shelley reciting the poems movingly and Janet directing. Both were professionals in theatre and film at the time, but this effort took place in a timeframe that preceded videotaped, narrated books. I called our 30-minute film "Look at the Book." Originally It was intended only as a promotion for the actual publication of *Altar Pieces*.

The idea was innovative at the time. In the course of my life, I have always been a little ahead of the curve in my creative efforts. Today I reflect that it makes things easier for public acceptance (and funding!) to come up with a transformative idea not more than five minutes or so before everyone else does. At an advanced age now—I recognize that I have moved from "aging" to "aged"—my pace and rhythm have slowed to the point where my energy is nearly normal, something I welcome, so long as I don't fall behind too much in this technological age.

In this 21st century, of course, we are used to reading books as e-books on our various online devices. Audiobooks are popular, especially to fill the time in a companionate way while driving. At home, I can even reach out to my virtual assistant, Alexa, and ask her to read my latest e-book (from the library, online) at bedtime. In fact, I was pleasantly surprised when I absent-mindedly thanked Alexa for her help, and, in return, the robotic voice effusively thanked me for my kindness. I also have my own virtual library of at least one hundred "keeper" books that I have purchased on my Kindle reader, and I am old-fashioned enough to have many, many shelves of much-loved books in print on my home office, bedroom, living room, and anywhere-else-I-can-put-them walls. There is something inspiring about having your own scribbled notes in the margin that make a book special every time you re-read it, with the feel of good paper every time you turn the page. I underline phrases or sentences that are meaningful to me. It's possible, of course, to do this in a computer-generated way too on my Kindle, but somehow it just isn't the same. Old habits die hard.

In any case, I envisioned the eventual production of *Altar Pieces* as a large coffee table book (a costly endeavor), but that was not to be. To my great surprise, when I offered the intended 30-minute promotion to a new Canadian TV network, Vision TV, one focused on educational and religious themes, the network (then connected with both the Learning and Discovery channels) not only leased it immediately, but response was so favorable that they continued to screen it (cut to 23 minutes to allow for commercials!) for five years.

Many years have gone by, and I still often find myself whispering the four short lines in *Altar Pieces* that represent my forever longing:

"Shall we first meet
In the middle of the air,
Shall I come to find
The sky within you there?"[3]

When I wrote these heartfelt words, they were part of an imagining, an unrequited searching for something that might not even exist. Yet, in 2023, in these first online decades of a still new century, it's not so hard to imagine the moment when two people searching urgently for their spiritual, and at times physical, counterpart might meet in the unknown clouds of possibility we currently call the Internet.

And maybe—who knows? —might even connect in their searching with something unseen, something we can't touch, something that, by different names, we call divine. Just as, years ago, I wrote this title poem to express that same feeling in *Embrace.*

Rabbi Corinne Copnick

EMBRACE

Wish a ring around your finger,

and I'll light you a place I've seen

where purple flashes shiver skull spaces,

where pastpresentfuture blind

together in one unbroken line

circling like a welded marriage band.

You may hold a lover there

And, gentling, find the lover in yourself.[4]

If we believe that possibilities we have only dreamed about can actually come into being— if we are willing not only to exercise our life-acquired knowledge and imagination, but also to keep our hopes alive when others may be skeptical, then…if we're willing to put in the effort and time and hard work to turn our dreams into reality even when there are setbacks, and if we believe that the unseen—what we don't know yet, what we can't physically touch— will help us in ways we can't yet understand in our own time, we are never too old to teach younger generations how to be hopeful too. We will have found the lover in ourselves and learned how to extend it to other people. What we need now is the will to continue. That is what this book is all about.

SECTION ONE

A PERSONAL PERSPECTIVE ON HOPE

In the Beginning: One-year-old Corinne holding a ball—and gaining a global perspective from the get-go. Photo taken in Montreal, Quebec by a family friend in 1937. (©Corinne Copnick, Los Angeles, 2023. All rights reserved.)

CHAPTER 1

THE WILL TO CONTINUE

$\mathcal{S}$oon after Richard Siegel and Rabbi Laura Geller's then newly published book, *Getting Good at Getting Older*, was available, I read it with great interest.[5] It's an excellent resource, beautifully designed with pages filled with helpful ideas and information about different organizations. In addition to the easy-to-read text, it's also peppered with humor and inspirational quotes. Its target audience, as Rabbi Geller acknowledges, is the boomer group, people now in their 60s (perhaps newly retired or considering retirement), and into the mid-seventies (for those who "boomed" earlier).

What *Getting Good at Getting Older* does not cover, though, are those who got older some time ago, those in their late 70s, 80s, and 90s. Some of them apparently got very good at getting older because, if you follow your local obituaries, you'll notice the growing number of people who have lived to pass the century mark.

In his gripping article, "A Secret Aging: How You Can Ward Off Death,"[6] Rabbi Bradley Shavit Artson notes that that even in the Middle Ages, Rabbi Ibn Ezra wrote about Moses and Aaron's old age in a complimentary fashion.[7] For Ibn Ezra, their advanced age as these leaders accomplished great deeds was a source of pride for *B'nai Israel* (the biblical children of Israel).

The Talmud tells us, as Rabbi Artson also mentions, that human destiny is to live to the age of three score and ten (70 years), but that those who have "strength" can live to 80. Thus 80 years is defined as the age of strength in the Talmud, and Artson defines this strength primarily as "the wisdom and compassion that comes from experience and completion…. At 80, we no longer serve either passion or ambition."[8]

In my own experience, since I have already had my 87th birthday, what Rabbi Artson says is largely true, but there is more. Granted there is the wisdom, understanding, compassion — and a sense of history, I would add — that comes from having lived a long time, with its accompanying ups and downs and even skepticism. But I disagree when it comes to people in their 80s no longer having the need to serve passion. In my view, it's the passion that keeps you going! Otherwise, you're in danger of folding up your personal tent.

Rabbi Abraham Joshua Heschel got it right when he wrote these words: "May I suggest that [human] potential for change and growth is much greater than we are willing to admit, and that old age… be regarded as the age of opportunities for inner growth."[9]

For me, the strength of living into one's 80s, and hopefully beyond, comes from the will to continue. It comes from believing you still have something to contribute, both concretely and by passing on your wisdom and experience (and money, if it hasn't run out and you still have some). If the younger generations are truly willing to listen and don't discard what you have to offer as irrelevant today, maybe your assistance will help them to achieve their goals in a world that has changed exponentially, not only with every generation but with every decade now. As for the boomers, they have already learned that paradoxical truth, "*plus ça change, plus c'est la même chose* (the more things change, the more they stay the same)."

My own four children, close together in age, are all tail-end baby boomers. I believe with all my heart that they will continue to succeed, continue to grow as they get older, that they will be good at it. And when, God willing, they reach "the age of strength," the age when Rabbi Artson says that younger people "can put off death by honoring the old among us,"[10] I hope they, too, when the time comes, will have the will to continue — with passion — beyond honor, beyond past achievement. Perhaps they will also have learned that no matter how smart we humans are, no matter how much we are assisted by continually advancing artificial intelligence, none of us truly knows what the future holds. That's God's job.

Since I'd like to elaborate on some of these thoughts, and my own time in this world, with my body and mind more or less intact, is getting closer to eventually running out, it's also time to put my will to continue on paper, or to be more precise on the computer screen. In other words, at my advanced age, as I write these words, I am strongly aware that I have the will to continue. Why? For my grandchildren I suppose, and for their children-to-be.

And for the grandkids and eventual great-grandkids of people I have never met as well. In other words, the contents of this book, like everything I have ever written, are an offering of love. That's why I believe that miracles, little miracles, not necessarily big miracles in the realm of the divine, yet big miracles too, are what you make of them.

As Albert Einstein has often been quoted, "There are only two ways to live: As though nothing is a miracle, or as though everything is a miracle."[11] Helping miracles come into being is also an act of love. And, taking it a step further, as I like to observe, "Miracles are what you make of them."

A Window to the Outside World

Over the past several years, Zoom online programming has been my own little miracle, my window to the outside world in effect. Like many of you, this new technology made the viewpoints of my colleagues and friends available to me in these difficult pandemic times. I learned so much from the thinking process and knowledge of others and offered my own as well. It enabled me to see friendly faces I know, as well as those new to me, in mosaic tiles. And on Zoom, we could actually "see" one another, full face, for a while. We didn't need masks when we were on the screen.

I have the good fortune to live with two of my grown children and one of my grandchildren already graduated from university as well. I do not have to watch television or have a Sabbath dinner alone. We have a beautiful garden in which to relax and have family meals outside. However, as a diabetic for the last 27 years, I do have a compromised immune system. So, during lockdown, I had listened faithfully to the advice of our California government and our dedicated health experts and remained mostly indoors since the beginning of March 2020. Apart from a daily walk around the block or so, and one quick visit to the beach on a day that it was "open," I had rarely been "outside" since the "stay safe at home" instruction was issued.

At first I watched a lot of television, especially the daily comments of New York governor Andrew Cuomo, whose service to our nation then, it should not be forgotten, was invaluable, (despite later "Me Too" accusations of aggressive sexual overtures in the workplace). As a family, we caught up on recent TV series with "binge-watching." We cooked and baked a lot. Courtesy of the Los Angeles library, I had read some fifty or so books online. Good books. I visited my doctors for online appointments when "telehealth" became readily available.

Perhaps most important, I included in my daily schedule attending at least one Zoom lecture or teaching on a particular topic every single day. When it became too overwhelming—and tiring as well, because learning on Zoom requires a constant, single-focus attention, I restricted my Zoom screen time to only one lecture a day. Gradually, I developed the confidence to successfully host and teach my own Zoom sessions for my *Beit Kulam* adult education classes.

And I am proud to have mastered, at least to some small extent, and an online class helped, a new technology that can be a very "cold" medium for teaching—unless you learn how to make it "warm." Recorded lectures tend to be on the cold side, and I have found that it's best to have shorter bursts of "teaching," with a lot of discussion, or guided discussion, and visuals to add interest, if possible, in between. Still so much to be learned about making use of our ever-growing technologies engagingly and productively.

When I virtually presented my new (2020) book, *A Rabbi at Sea* in New York for the Jewish Book Council network, I saw how meticulous preparation and engagement could make a large-scale event very successful. Where there's a will—and a need that could otherwise be overwhelming—there's a way!

* * * *

In the meantime, until recently when I started to write *Miracles Are What You Make of Them*, for the last decade I have made myself available to my *Beit Kulam*[12] members (a twice monthly study group I started in 2014 as a Sunday morning breakfast club), and on Friday afternoons for two years I virtually taught a weekly private Torah class to my own daughter and her non-Jewish partner in Vancouver. It has proved to be both a beautiful and calming experience before greeting *Shabbat*. Their "homework" was to read various commentaries about each week's *parsha* (weekly portion from the Bible) before we read it aloud together. We also gave the gift of increasing strength to one another by reciting the traditional "*Hazak, hazak, v'nitkazek*"[13] as each book of the five books of the Torah concluded. When we finished Deuteronomy, the last of the five, which largely summarizes what has happened in the previous four books, it was an especially joyful moment as we congratulated and even mimed hugging one another virtually.

So, for some people, the rapidly changing new technologies drive them nuts. And sometimes I am one of those people. Usually, though, it has been a wonderful way to preserve my sanity amidst the labyrinth of dark and conflicting news broadcasts that now permeate our wonderful world. For me, the new technologies, bringing with them exposure to many points of views, are a saving grace. Can I help it if I'm naturally hopeful and optimistic?

I remember the devastating polio epidemic of my youth that so badly affected my mother's cousin, Libby (*Libbele* in Yiddish), that she was paralyzed from the waist down for the rest of her life, confined to a wheelchair. But she had an indomitable spirit. She mastered many crafts, through which she made a small living, and her loving relatives made sure she was well supported, emotionally and financially, throughout her life.

Like the many other pandemics that permeate our world history (one of the four disasters that the Jewish holiday, *Tisha B'Av*, memorializes is the plague that killed 24,000 students of Rabbi Akivah[14]), it was eventually thousands of years later when Dr. Jonas Salk developed a vaccine.[15] As I write this, our scientists around the world have been working furiously to find the right vaccines to overcome our current plague, Covid-19, with all its mutant variations. With God's help, they will continue to do so, and, as second stage polio and even some newly emergent cases of polio (previously considered conquered) has become a concern, they will continue the medical quest. As Dr. Salk is famously quoted, "Hope lies in dreams, in imagination and in the courage of those who dare to make dreams into reality."[16]

"I am a rabbi, one who came to that calling at a late age. In fact, I graduated from rabbinical school and was ordained at the age of 79 after six years of intensive study. I believe in the Judaic purpose "to do" in accordance with a moral code intended to be both particular and universal. Our laws are supposed to be particular to Jews, who in turn, by their behavior will be a light unto the nations; that is, set an example of moral behavior accompanied by fruitful actions that will encourage other peoples to do the same. "Believe in God because God is good." God is *"tov"* (good). Think *"tov,"* do *"tov"* (to yourself and others). Study why we do *"tov."* Study how to do more *"tov."* That is our moral code in brief.

The difficulty is interpreting what is "good," something we have debated in our Talmud, in our houses of study, in our congregations, in our hearts and souls, for thousands of years. And now, in our open society, many people have been asking, "Is everything relative, a moral equivalent? The global looming shifts in democracy and disturbing moves to autocracy are a double trend upsetting long-held values.

So my continuing question is this: What's good? *Mah tovu?"*[17]

> "He has told you, O man, what is good.
>
> And what the Lord requires of you:
>
> Only to do justice,
>
> And to love goodness,
>
> And to walk modestly with your God."
>
> (Micah 6: 8-12)[18]

CHAPTER 2

THE WILL TO HOPE

THE WILL TO HOPE

Ehyeh asher Ehyeh (I will be what I will be)[19]

"Judaism, the religion of hope, is faith in the future tense."
—Rabbi Jonathan Sacks[20]

I am especially dedicating this chapter, "The Will to Hope," to the resilience of my grandchildren's generation, afflicted with a plague that won't go away. At my grandson's graduation (B.Sc. majoring in Cognitive Systems, with a Neuroscience focus) last spring from the prestigious University of British Columbia in Vancouver, Canada, the Rector noted the remarkable persistence and resilience of the graduating class. ("The most resilient graduating class we have ever had," he said, praising their determination to travel and to make the world a better place.) This is Generation Z. My granddaughter also graduated (B.A. majoring in Environmental Studies and Sociology) with the same high hopes, from the University of California in Santa Barbara.

I am hopeful for this generation too. Certainly, anyone who saw the impressive images (both televised and available online) produced in 2022 in full color by the new James Webb Telescope, could not fail to be hopeful. It was a mind-blowing, world-changing astronomical experience that left me gasping in amazement as I viewed "unprecedented observations of the birth of stars and the formation of galaxies."[21]

Dark Matter, Dark Energy, and *Ein Sof*

In the television presentation, the earth appeared as a tiny dot at the edge of our galaxy in a vast universe animated by a dark energy that science does not understand as yet, but scientists do know it is an energy that never stops creating, never stops expanding. Although the television commentary went beyond what I, a non-scientist, could completely understand, it seems to me that science is coming very close to approaching *Ein Sof*, a biblical Hebrew phrase for God, indeed one of the many names for God. (It means "there is no end.")

From what I gleaned from the television commentaries and short articles I have read or listened to, the dark matter and dark energy scientists have identified in the universe seem to be two very different things. However, scientists are not sure exactly what dark matter is; apparently, they mostly know what it is NOT.

One of the simplest definitions I could find reads as follows: "Dark matter is the mysterious stuff that fills the universe, but no one has ever seen." Furthermore, this unseeable dark matter fills a considerable percent of the universe, according to NASA's current scientific assessment.[22] So scientists do know that dark matter is abundant in the universe and that "it has a strong influence on its structures and evolution."[23]

Another simple definition from *Oxford Languages*, also found online, reads as follows: "According to cosmological theory, soon after the Big Bang [hot dark matter], cold matter formed the universe's first large-scale structures, which then collapsed under their own weight to form lost halos."[24]

So how do we humans know that dark matter, which can't be explained by currently accepted theories of gravity, really exists? Here's another try at defining it, which I also found by questioning the Internet:

"Dark matter is composed of particles that do not absorb, reflect, or emit light, so they cannot be detected by observing electric magnetic radiation." Dark matter can't even be seen directly, but we know that it exists. How? Because of its effect on objects that we can't observe directly.[25]

In my baby-step layman's terms, from what I have read or listened to, this is a brief summary of what is understood about dark matter as I write this in early 2023.

Also, scientists currently think that further knowledge about dark energy, like dark matter, may even contradict some of Einstein's theories about gravity. (Sorry, Einstein!). As Bill Nye, "the Science Guy," put it so succinctly in an interview on CNN recently, "Dark matter is gravity, and dark energy pushes that gravity around."[26] So dark energy is a force that pushes back against gravity—it repulses gravity—and thus expands the universe continuously over time.[27] In other words, it continues creating forever.

For me, this is a mind-boggling discovery: a scientific confirmation that there is indeed an everlasting force, one that even our finest minds do not understand completely, that exists in our universe, and it keeps on creating forever. One might say that, in the twenty-first century, science is putting God back in the sky. It underlines the Judaic belief system transmitted for thousands of years: The Creator is forever. A manifestation of *Ein Sof* is indeed eternal. There is a spiritual, as well as earthly, reason to hope. So much to think about. So much to learn.

The personal side of our God-given selves must also be taken into account, especially when it affects the next generation, our children. When Rabbi Bradley Shavit Artson,[28] Dean of the Ziegler Rabbinic School in Los Angeles, was devastated by the diagnosis of his son's autism, it took him a decade of reckoning with God before he was able to develop a different understanding of God that he calls "process thought."[29]

According to Rabbi Artson, "everything is in the process of becoming, and every process—you, me, the world, the cosmos, God—is not a substance, a thing, but rather a distinctive pattern of energy that retains some measure of constancy in the midst of change and growth."[30]

As Artson further explains, 1) the possibility for change is always present; and 2) both human beings and the world we inhabit are in a state of continual *becoming*. This is essentially the Talmud's position on hope, too, one that empowers the journey between hope and despair on both a personal and societal level.

I first started thinking about the Jewish emphasis on "becoming" when I began my study of the Hebrew language at age 73 and discovered that there is no present tense in Hebrew in the way we know it in English. Rather, the present is a gerund, an "ing," a movement from past to future, with the present in between. The present, in effect, serves as a "becoming" for everyone, also in both personal and societal terms. In that sense, it is an important tool for empowerment and action in the face of despair.

* * * *

To get back to this world that we live in at the present time, I began this book by musing about the "Will to Continue" in my senior years. The corollary to maintaining that will-power is the "Will to Hope." In my view, as you know by now, the journey to get to age ninety—or even one hundred these days, from that biblical age of strength, the eighties, requires an act of will. Increasingly, as I write these pages, I find myself hoping for good things and believing they will come—not only for myself, but also for others, both in my personal circles and beyond. And for our world, that little dot in the universe, perhaps the meta-universe.

Of course, this subjugation of self is mitigated by the reality that I am not only Mind, I am also a Physical Self, thankfully one currently in reasonable health with some intervening intervals. And although I don't usually admit it to anyone, I am forgetful more often than I would like.

While a little nostalgia is a good thing, as the Shalom Hartman Institute's Rabbi Joshua Ladon pointed out in his 2022 pre-High Holiday Workshop address to the Board of Rabbis of Southern California,[31] it's important to use the memories and knowledge to move forward. So here goes:

Some thirty-seven years ago, when I was only in my fifties, there was some awareness of a difference between what was then termed "the Young-Old" (60 to 75) and "the Old-Old" (over 75). With the Baby Boomers dominant (over 50 became the pathway to "freedom"), few people dared to say "golden ager" or "senior citizen" anymore. The "Young-Old" could do many more things physically than the "Old-Old," and even (with eye lifts and face lifts and exercise and yoga classes) did not even seem to be past a youthful middle age, if you weren't really looking that hard. However, at present, with people living so much longer, unless they have succumbed to the pandemic, there are also the "Very-Old" (over 85, most of whom are presumed to have some form of dementia, even if they don't, or, in the case of pandemics, have already become an integral part of our throw-away culture). In my euphoric moments, I call myself "Chronologically Enriched," a recommendation from my creative daughter, Susan. Lately I have been referring to myself as a "Vintage Original."

As we have seen when medical facilities are overwhelmed, the embrace of a triage culture is rather scary if indeed you are already in an elderly category with serious medical deficits. It's hard to decide what to do when resources are limited.

What does Judaism say about this dilemma? The various Jewish denominations have different takes on it but recognize the biblical wisdom enunciated in *Ecclesiastes 3:2a*: "There is a time to live and a time to die."[32] While usually the Jewish tradition weighs the scales heavily in the direction of life, an important distinction is made between the prolongation of human life, on the one hand, and the prolongation of the death process on the other—a sensitive issue discussed later in this book.[33]

As the baseball player Yogi Berra was often quoted as saying, "It ain't over until it's over."[34]

While we are in the land of the living, there are still contributions we can make to fill societal and workplace needs, but on an adjusted calendar. I'm not talking about volunteer work. We seniors already do plenty of that. Nonetheless, it's very comforting to have a paycheck at a certain age when you don't know how much longer your savings will last. Or if inflation is eating them up faster than what you can afford to buy at the grocery store—or when luxury "active senior communities" (on a sliding scale of accommodation depending on your finances, state of health, and actual ability to look after yourself), and even less fancy facilities, are priced beyond your expectations or possibilities to consider.

Suppose you are a Vintage Original like me, not a baby boomer. Your hard-earned, long-saved money is not worth what you thought it would be when you finally retired. Long gone is the expectation that your "investments," some of which disappeared in the 2008 stock market crash (or in the exchange from Canadian to U.S. dollars), can cover what you essentially need when you are very old. At least, if you were smart, you purchased a cemetery plot when they were still affordable. Otherwise, your family may have to opt for an urn for your ashes.

Although I don't usually tell anyone except my family this (except now I'm confiding in you): I have signed the medical form that declines resuscitation or to be put on a ventilator should I fall dangerously ill in this time of possibly multiple pandemics. I don't want to leave my loved ones with a burden that won't go away instead of a person they love. While none of us know at any age when our time is up, it's best to be prepared. (When I was a kid, Brownies and Scouts were popular activities and emphasized good values: "Be Prepared" is still the Scout motto—and it's still mine.)

I have to admit that sometimes I too have bleak thoughts, along with the memory of my mother who cared for my gravely ill father for twenty-seven years. During most of them he remained in a vegetative or semi-vegetative state, until he finally died. One of my daughters is also a caretaker now, although to a much lesser degree, for her much-loved husband, Ira: He has survived a brain tumor that would not bow to the diagnosis of fast-approaching terminal cancer, and, at this writing is thankfully still with us after twelve years of continued treatments and respites.

Yes, he did lose the ability to do some of the things that he loved doing, but he replaced them with something truly wonderful: He created an informational social media presence with many thousands of followers for brain cancer survivors. In this way, he helped many cancer patients around the world. In addition, he created an online forum in memory of his late brother, David Brown, an artist lost to cancer, his life and talent cut short. Years later, visitors can still enjoy the fruits of his abstract visual art on the Internet.

As for my son-in-law, he spends many of his days in his music studio, reworking some of the 200 songs he has written in his lifetime and writing new ones too. His talent has not been lost. And, miraculously, this man who was told he would likely die within a few months is still in the land of the living and has helped many others along the way.

Both my daughter and son-in-law have recently entered their sixties—and they have never, ever relinquished hope in whatever the future might turn out to be. They have seen their son, Joshua, a university graduate now, currently exploring and engaging his artistic interests; and their daughter, Rachel, gifted both artistically and musically, has graduated from high school and is presently studying vocal arts as a university music major and working on her own compositions. My daughter, Shelley, has continued her work as a talented Interior Designer. And so life continues.

What I have learned over the years is this: Keeping hopeful in one's late eighties and nineties and maybe beyond, requires an act of faith, of faith in the future, not only for oneself but also for others—especially for our family members, now grown, and for the grandchildren and great grandchildren yet to be born, and, yes, for our own continuance in their memories and that of our ancestors through the generations. When my children were young, I expressed these hopes in poetry:

CONTINUITY[5]

Beyond the simple, repetitive cycle
are thematic mutations
uniquely conceived to alter slightly
familiar stains and hues,

color the vacuum with multi-dyed pattern,
limited edition found on faith
and acid-etched on a limestone block,
each reprint adding new dimensions
to the composite
before it is sanded down, re-used,
a statement washed away.

A single lithograph preserved
brightens walls where my children
grease pencil personal
drawings, blueprinting continuity
for the next generation.

    —Corinne Copnick

Why is this poem still so important to me today? Probably it's because this expression of poetic optimism embraces hope, not only for the people I love, but also for the world—and the people who inhabit it. I want it to extend beyond my own personal world. I would dearly love to be here to see what else the latest telescope will reveal to us.

Yet, as I write these lines, we are just beginning to realize that previously unknown illnesses are likely to discover us—just like measles and smallpox decimated native populations unfamiliar with these diseases as much of the New World was being colonized by Europeans centuries ago. Now we have monkeypox, a possible resurgence of polio and antibiotic-resistant fungus to worry about.

The Europeans themselves had received the unwelcome gift of these new diseases from conquering Roman soldiers in other far-away lands, whose infected people probably got it from animals unfamiliar to their own part of the world. Somehow the world goes on, thankfully aided, if not sufficiently by the science of the day, by the science of the future. And yes, by faith.

I believe with all my heart that everything we need is already here on earth, all the knowledge, every cure, every invention, in the beautiful world we inhabit, one I think we may have hopefully discovered it is foolish to recklessly deplete.

As the great astronomer Carl Sagan wrote in 1990, when images from an earlier different telescope were released, "To me it underscores our responsibility to deal kindly with one another and to preserve and cherish the pale blue dot…. That's the only home we have ever known."[36]

Thirty-two years later, in July, 2022, when the newly released NASA images took us back "13.2 billion years to when the universe was new," the *CNN Morning Brew* columnist observed, "What a privilege it is to be alive."[37]

What A Privilege It Is To Be Alive!

We have only to discover it, generation by generation, intelligence building on intelligence, faith building on faith, and— eventually, every few centuries, put two and two together, at least for a while, until some new discovery stirs our instincts to move in still unexplored directions. So once again, thank you, God. Thank you, Eternal Energy—*Ein Sof,* as the Jewish people have called You for thousands of years. While, as I mentioned earlier, literally it means "there is no end," in English we usually refer to it as *"Eternal."*

Eternal…with what we humans call an intelligence so huge and a desire to keep creating forever so vast that even our greatest scientists don't understand it yet. But they know it's there. And now we humbler human beings know that too. We are learning what the mystics have sensed through the ages. The Forever is always there. Creation never stops.

More than three-quarters of a century ago, in his classic book, *The Sabbath*, one of Judaism's great thinkers, Rabbi Abraham Joshua Heschel, expanded his understanding of the act of creation as continual in these words: "Time is perpetual innovation, a synonym for continuous creation, God's gift to the world of space...the secret of being is the eternal within time."[38]

It gives me spinal shivers just to put these words into my book.

One of my favorite references, the late Lord Rabbi Jonathan Sacks, explains this concept in simpler words. "Judaism, the religion of hope, is faith in the future tense."[39] The World-to-Come of the Talmud is not yet here, so we have to keep striving, every generation, to make the world better. "To be a Jew is to be an agent of hope in a world serially threatened by despair," Sacks concludes.[40] On the other hand, sometimes I think mankind has never learned the biblical lesson of the biblical Tower of Babel story.[41] Maybe we can raise our collective hand in the hope of meeting the metaphorical hand of God halfway between heaven and earth, but we also would be well advised not to over-reach. We are not gods; we are human beings whose ambitions have sometimes *gang aft agley* (gone astray) as the poet Robbie Burns put it.[42] We humans are already polluting space with blown-up bits of rockets and other detritus. It's time for morality and ethics and just plain common sense to come into the mix. Now.

The Torah, that interpreter of *Ein Sof* 's instruction (and perhaps even serving as God's biographer at times)[43] has endured in large part because it is believed to provide human beings with a divinely inspired blueprint for how to lead a moral life, an ethical life. History has taken humanity, and, in particular, the Jewish people, down diverse roads to far-flung places over the millennia. Customs have changed, ideas have been dissected, and new ones introduced time and again, yet the ethical map of permissible actions, while continually rethought in the light of new knowledge and generational change, remains basically the same.

And something else remains the same throughout the ages. Something very important that supersedes new knowledge. We continue to love one another. In Your name. You're a good influence, God. You fill us with great energy! And, in an age when "streaming" agents dominate our TV and computer screens, You have taught us for centuries through stories.

Your Torah, in fact, is full of dramatic stories, and the Talmud abounds in stories about little acts of kindness. So does our rabbinic literature across the centuries. Maybe that's why I'm a storyteller too. So let me tell another story, a true story that I wrote about something that happened to me and altered my perception of the world ever after. It's called "The Guarantors." [44] You'll find it in the next chapter.

CHAPTER 3

WHEN LITTLE MIRACLES HAPPEN

THE GUARANTORS

WHEN THE FATWA GENERATED A STORM

THE GUARANTORS

*P*ersonally, I have always had the utmost respect for the prophets who spoke out against the dictums of the Torah being broken. Great prophets like Isaiah, Ezekiel, and Jeremiah all suffered consequences for their honesty, their outspokenness, and their dramatic actions, which, in some instances, rivaled the street theatre of activist Alan Ginsberg and his ilk in the 1960s. These ancient prophets had no television, no 21st century Internet, texting, tweets, or other Social Media channels to communicate their unpopular messages to the people. They had to use more primitive methods: wearing an ox yoke to symbolize commitment to the Torah, posting messages on the Temple door, or staging what we would call a hunger strike today beside the Chabar Canal. The prophets were indeed guarantors of the Torah. Keep the commandments, they preached in their various ways, and fearlessly they rebuked the Jewish people in no uncertain terms, predicting dire consequences for straying from the covenant. But they also offered hope and consolation to those who returned to the Torah.

Today each of us who identify as Jews are also guarantors of the Torah, and hopefully we will have children who will want to be Jewish and to be guarantors of the Torah too. Even more hopefully, we will have sufficient children to guarantee the continuity of the

Jewish people. In the final analysis, we — each of us — are what our grandchildren will be.

In my most optimistic moments, I like to recall the legend of the *Lamed Vavs*—that if there are only thirty-six righteous people in the four corners of the world, the world will be upheld, and we will always be alright. As individuals, we can't always affect the course of history, or uphold the world by ourselves, but we can do little things that add up to a lot. In the spirit of the Torah, we can do little acts of kindness.

My father believed in the chain of goodness: that if you do a kind thing for someone, that person will do a kind thing for someone else, and thus the chain of goodness continues, unbroken. You are standing at Sinai. In contemporary terms, they call it "paying it forward."

That's what this story is all about. It's a story that actually began long ago.

Yet sometimes a story can be just one line. I once read a single headline in a Jewish newspaper. In big, black letters, it said: "You are what your grandchildren are." Whoo! Plenty of drama there. Just in that one sentence. But you have to fill in the gaps with your own imagination.

So let me tell you that long ago story, one that affected me personally, and that I still think about often. It appears in a well-known *midrash* (commentary) on the biblical "Song of Songs" found in "The Song of Songs *Rabbah*" (1-24). It first caught my attention in Joseph Telushkin's subsequent commentary in *Jewish Literacy*, and I want to share it with you.

As the biblical people of Israel assembled at Sinai to receive the Torah, God explained that he would grant them the gift of the Torah provided that they would give him dependable guarantors to guard it with great care. The Israelites thoughtfully considered this request and suggested that their patriarchs would be good guarantors. However, the patriarchs were not acceptable to God as guarantors. So the people came back with another suggestion. Wouldn't the prophets be good guarantors? Once again, God refused this offer.

"Finally, they say, 'Behold, our children are our guarantors.' And God responds, 'They are certainly good guarantors. For their sake, I give the Torah to you.'"[45]

And now this long ago story becomes our story. I call it "The Guarantors." Each of us reading this story who identify as Jews are guarantors of the Torah, and hopefully some of us will have children who will want to be Jewish and to be guarantors of the Torah too. Even more hopefully, we will have sufficient children to guarantee the continuity of the Jewish people. And maybe they will have children. Our grandchildren.

We are what our grandchildren are.

And now this becomes my story, a true story, a grandmother's story that I especially want to share with you. When I think of little acts of kindness, I often think of the young *Hasid* (ultra-Orthodox Jew) who drove me home in a blizzard when I lived in Toronto. I had bought my Toronto home in a mainly modern Orthodox area because I didn't know if I would like the more conservative Toronto after the elegant, exuberant, francophone culture of Montreal, but I did know that I would always be able to sell a home that was within walking distance of so many synagogues. It was also close to the highway so that I could drive back to Montreal if I missed the city of my birth too much. In those days, we referred to Toronto as "Toronto the Good."

But it turned out to be very nice where I lived. I really liked Toronto a lot. The garden of my house backed onto a lovely park that was very quiet during the week, but on Saturday summer and autumn afternoons, I loved watching the modern Orthodox families walking together in the park. Once I watched a father teaching his bar-mitzvah-aged son to waltz on the park's pathways.

Then suddenly it was winter, and the park was blanketed with snow. One night I drove home from a social gathering around midnight. I should have known better. The falling snowflakes had already grown into a raging blizzard. My car made uneasy noises to show that this was not a night to be driving. And sure enough, about fifteen or twenty blocks from my street, my car conked out.

No way to start it, no how! It was completely dead. Cell phones had not yet been invented, so I couldn't call for help. I couldn't walk home; it was too far to go in the blinding blizzard, and I couldn't stay in the car. Without heat, I would freeze to death. My windows were already frosted over, and my car completely covered with snow.

I was loathe to knock on a stranger's door after midnight. What to do? I decided to stand outside right beside the car in the hope that someone would soon drive by on the deserted street. Smart people were inside.

Finally, as I was beginning to shiver and shake with the cold, despite my warm clothing, a big, black station wagon came to a halt beside me. Driving it was a young *Hasid*.[46] "Do you need help?" he asked. He tried valiantly to start my car, but it was no use.

"I'll have to leave the car here," I said. "I just live a few blocks from here. About fifteen. Do you think you could drive me home?"

He looked very uncomfortable, and I realized that he did not like the idea of being alone in a car with a woman. He tucked his side-curls behind his ears. But, as the blizzard whirled around us, he swallowed his misgivings and squeaked, "Sure. Hop in."

Very carefully, looking straight ahead through the window and not at me, and not saying a word, he slowly drove me home. As I got out of the car, I thanked him profusely. It was pitch dark outside, but I think he blushed. "Thank you for giving me the opportunity to do a *mitzvah*," he replied. He was perhaps the age of my grandchildren.

As we looked at one another, two Jews whose backgrounds were so different, our eyes locked in a moment of understanding. A *mitzvah*.[47] A little act of kindness. Of course. We knew immediately that we were witnesses. We had seen one another at Sinai.[48] We would continue. We were Guarantors.

"See you at Sinai," I said softly in parting.

****

When the Fatwa Generated a Storm:
More Little Miracles

I've often thought that we don't always recognize the little miracles that keep happening in our lives. Since I'm originally from Montreal in Canada, I have experienced a lot of snow in my own life. So, in recognition of all the little miracles, "When the Fatwa Generated a Storm" describes how yet another little miracle happened in a snowstorm. Then it was compounded by yet another little miracle—and another. In fact, little miracles are happening all the time. We just don't notice them.

My late sister, who lived in upper New York State, was confined to a wheelchair for many years and so was able to visit my mother and myself, still living in Toronto, only rarely. But in that particular year, my sister felt well enough to visit me to celebrate my birthday. It was December, 1992 when she arrived, more than a quarter of a century ago.

Thrilled that she was coming, I had planned various activities I knew she would enjoy, among them PEN Canada's annual gala, a fund-raiser at which some of PEN's literary celebrities (like Margaret Atwood) would perform.[49] The event was to be held at the magnificent, downtown Pantages Theatre in Toronto, where I reserved two seats, one of them wheelchair accessible for my sister, with great sightlines. But the night of the gala, it started to snow hard, quite hard, and so I packed my sister into the car, folded her wheelchair into the trunk, and, in order to get there on time, left much earlier than I would have done normally.

Canadian born, my sister and I were used to winter. I know how to drive in snow. My family were all skiers. But this night was a doozer! Despite the weather, though, when we got to the theatre, it was packed full of hardy souls, just as we expected. Firstly, the tickets were too expensive not to come, once you had one, and secondly, none of the assembled *literati*, including me, were going to miss the PEN gala. It was not exactly the Canadian version of the Oscars, but it was close.

My sister's handicap placard wasn't valid in Canada, but the police—oh my goodness, there seemed to be a lot of them! – kindly let me park right in front of the theatre long enough to unpack the wheelchair and push my sister, a rather hefty bundle, through the snow into the theatre. We found her seat, and then I left to park my car.

By this time, the snow was heavy but still "walkable," and I was exuberant at finding a parking space in a lot a couple of blocks away, or so it seemed to me. I quickly parked the car and briskly walked back to the theatre, sinking into my seat just a couple of minutes before the curtains parted for the show.

Nevertheless, I still had time to observe that the theatre's interior seemed to be lined with quite a few Mounties (Royal Canadian Mounted Police, although they rarely ride horses anymore) in full ceremonial dress. These are the federal police in Canada. Interspersed among them were others in civilian dress, detectives I thought, scrutinizing the crowd. And then I had no more time to think. The show had started!

It was a lot of fun, especially for people with a literary bent. My sister loved it. But then, just as the audience was starting to applaud for what we thought was the final curtain, a male figure strode onto the stage, surrounded by a semi-circle of Mounties.

The First Little Miracle

When the center figure of the semi-circle on the stage was introduced as Salman Rushdie, author of the satirical novel, *The Satanic Verses*, the audience gasped. We all knew that a *"fatwa"* calling for Rushdie's assassination had been issued by Ayatollah Ruhollah Khomeini, the Supreme Leader of Iran, four years earlier in 1989. Why? For satirizing the prophet Mohammed and his wife, Aisha, in *The Satanic Verses.* The Ayatollah considered it blasphemous. Salman Rushdie was therefore condemned to death, and anyone who murdered him would be well rewarded with a million-dollar bounty.[50]

But Salman Rushdie was British-Indian, born in India, educated at Cambridge, and a British citizen. For the Ayatollah to issue a death warrant for a British subject was a great affront, not only to Britain, but to what was then called the free world—in other words, the West—whose shocked reaction was ineffective. Although Iran had thrown down the gauntlet, the Western countries seemed not to know what to do beyond diplomatic protests. Meanwhile there were public burnings of Rushdie's books in countries with Muslim majorities.

As a result, Rushdie was put under police protection by the British government for several years. The PEN event in Canada three years after the fatwa was issued marked the first time any organization had the courage to invite him to give a public reading.[51]

It took a great deal of courage and detailed planning, and the invitation was conducted in complete secrecy. Only the top executive leaders of PEN knew Rushdie was coming.

Onstage, an immensely grateful Rushdie described what it was like to live in hiding, fleeing with his wife, and—with the help of the British government—to sleep in a different house every night, and always with the fear of being killed in his sleep.

When Rushdie read to us excerpts from his new manuscript, *Midnight's Children*, which he was still writing while in hiding, it was a moment that neither Rushdie nor this 1992 audience would ever forget. Neither would the Premier of Ontario, Bob Rae, "who became the first head of government in the world to welcome him to a public forum." According to the PEN Newletter, it was such a memorable event, accompanied by tumultuous applause, that in 2012, PEN Canada held a 20th Anniversary celebration of this occasion.[52]

After the reading, my sister's face was flushed with excitement and appreciation. When Rushdie had first appeared on the stage, the audience had almost collapsed in, as one writer put it, "collective disbelief." It seemed like a miracle. For my sister and me, it was to be only the first miraculous event of the evening.

The Second Little Miracle

The second miracle didn't feel like a miracle at first. It felt more like a disaster. After I parked my sister in the theatre lobby in front of a large glass window looking out at the street, I said, "I'm going to get the car now. I won't be long. I'm just parked a couple of blocks away."

But when I stepped outside, the driving snow had turned into a veritable blizzard, and the direction I was walking was heading right into it. The snow had already built up halfway to my knees. So I crouched down low, lifting one foot up from the thick snow and planting it down further ahead in more thick snow, and then the same thing with the other foot. Methodically I advanced toward the parking lot a couple of blocks away. On the Southeast corner of the street, right? That's what I had noted when I originally parked there just two and a half hours earlier.

When I finally plodded through the snow to the parking lot on the corner, it was still full of cars. Only they all looked the same. Completely covered with snow. And guess what color my car was? You guessed it! White. Never buy a white car in Canada. I tried to determine the approximate place in which I had parked my car—and brushed away the snow from the license plates in that general area. Brush, brush! Not my car. Brush, brush! Not my car. After a lot of brush, brushing and many wrong license plates, I determined that 1) my car was not in that parking lot, no way, and 2) that I had better get back to the theatre lobby before they closed, and my sister was out in the street.

Plod, plod, plod, plod. "I'll never make it to the theatre." I was shivering. Just at that moment, I spotted an ambulance, a police ambulance, parked at the side of the road and just starting up the engine. "Wait, wait," I yelled at the top of my lungs. "Wait for me."

The ambulance driver did. I managed to reach his window and begged him to 1) help me pick up my invalid sister and 2) help me find my lost car. "Well, it's against the regulations" he hemmed and hawed, but as he watched my tears freeze on my face, he said, "Okay. Get in. I'll help you."

So we got my sister, to the worried manager's relief, and the three of us lifted the wheelchair, and my sister in it, into the ambulance. Thank God. My sister could not conceal her amazement. Where had this ambulance come from? I realized it had been parked on the street as a precaution in case there were any problems associated with the Rushdie reading. Well, now we were the problem, my sister and I.

"Show me this parking lot," the ambulance driver said kindly.

"The Southeast corner, two blocks down." So he drove me there, and I told him about my earlier brush, brush routine. He understood. "A white car," he groaned. His ambulance was white too. White and blue.

"You know," he said, "there's actually another parking lot on the Southeast corner, but it's one block over to the right. Do you think you could have parked there?"

A light went on in my head. Could it be?

So he drove us to the next lot, and after a lot of brush, brush on my part, the letters and numbers of my totally snow-covered license were revealed. My car! My white car!

We thanked him a million times as he transferred my sister to my car, helped me fold up the wheelchair and pack it in the trunk. Then he waited until I cleared the snow off my windows, the front and rear lights, and my tailpipe, revved up the car, and backed out. Ready to go.

"Drive slowly," he said. And with a wave of his hand, the officer and his ambulance were gone.

My sister and I were giddy with relief. We laughed and laughed and giggled and giggled. We couldn't stop. "No one will believe me," my sister chortled. She was known to embellish a tale or two. And then there was a third miracle.

The third miracle was that by keeping my eyes focused on the red tail lights of the cars directly in front of me, I managed to see my way through the blizzard. When we got home, we were still laughing.

So that's how it happened. Three miraculous events in one night. And all of them were generated by the courageous leadership of Canadian writers who respected the integrity and freedom of the pen. Even in a snowstorm.[53]

SECTION TWO

CONTEMPORARY JUDAIC CONCEPTS OF HOPE

Rabbi Corinne Copnick's *Rabbinic Ordination speech at age 79. The Academy for Jewish Religion 2015 graduation ceremony was at Stephen Wise Temple, Los Angeles, California in 2015. (Photo J. Spiegel, ©, Los Angeles, 2015.)*

CHAPTER 4

A GARDEN OF RABBINIC VIEWS

*O*ne late afternoon a few years ago[54], as I was driving home from *Ohr HaTorah*, the Los Angeles synagogue where I was interning (with Rabbi Mordecai Finley, one of the founders of the Academy for Jewish Religion California), I suddenly spotted a beautiful piece of lace, an antique lace fragment lying on the floor of my car. Dotted with opalescent sequins that resembled the re-embroidered lace decorating my long-ago wedding dress, it sparkled in the rays of sunshine that beamed through the car windows. When, at the next corner, I looked again, a coral-colored silk lining, barely showing itself where the corner of the antique lace turned back, pulsated like a beating heart. To me, it was not just a relic of the past; it seemed alive. My own heart pounding, I stopped the car at the first opportunity and reached for the lovely fragment, but then, like a mirage, it disappeared. My thoughts were playing tricks on me.

"That mirage is a representation of hope," I thought, "a glimpse of hope, ephemeral, combining past memories and future joys." And I knew I had to start writing my book while the symbolic image danced in my head. And, although I was not yet a Rabbi—I would not be ordained until 2015—I understood that, just maybe, this glimpse was my Call, my Call to service. Could it be?

"...I have singled you out by name,
You are Mine.

When you pass through water,

I will be with you;

Through streams,

They shall not overwhelm you.

When you walk through fire,

You shall not be scorched

Through flame,

It shall not burn you....″[55]

These words of God as they appear in Isaiah 43:1-8 are intended to reassure us, to give us hope in times of despair. Once these words were not yet written in a book or scroll. They were spoken by a great prophet, their wisdom memorized and handed down from generation to generation. And each generation has added its own wisdom, particular to its circumstances.

In contemporary circumstances, Rabbi Irving Greenberg expresses the traditional view so beautifully in his book, *Faith, Hope, and Redemption*[56]: "Hope is the vision of redemption; covenant is the process; faith is the covenantal commitment to realize the dream."

Yet each generation has wondered: Can you take hold of hope before, like a mirage, an illusion, it disappears? Is it made of different components, like the old lace, the old memories, and the new silk lining, meant for a future yet-to-come? Does it end when the vehicle of your life comes to a stop? Does it suddenly reappear when you least expect it?

We Jews have a vast literature about hope, from the biblical Psalms through the "World-to- Come" of the Talmud—but the Talmud does not envision hope in the modern context, but rather in a much larger time span—as Redemption for the Righteous (those who live a righteous life) in a future world (yet there is no single word for hope in the Talmud in the way we understand it today).

And through the huge number of Jewish texts that represent our continuing heritage right up to the Zionist impetus of our re-established Israel's anthem, *Hatikvah*, which actually means hope, we're still writing. Among other things, about hope.

For one thing, as the *Pirke Avot* ("The Ethics of the Fathers," an early tractate of *Mishnah* with many words of wisdom) makes clear, hope is something we must never give up, but, just to be on the safe side:

"Keep away from a bad neighbor.
And don't get involved with a bad person."[57]

Nevertheless, if you've been wronged, "don't give up hope [v'al titayesh] of retribution." [58]

Although these warnings do not fit the positive image suggested by the mirage of my lace fragment, the conclusion is the same: Do not give up hope. And now in 2023, still in the midst of continuing crises—a pandemic that won't quit; political infighting; an escalating war that threatens to become World War III—what I call "the horrible news," even as I am glued to the television or computer screen—I believe that past kindnesses will also be repaid, even generations later.

Yet there are skeptics. "Is hope the same thing as optimism?" they ask. Sigmund Freud would argue that certain aspects of hope are not psychologically healthy, that they encourage illusion as a form of wishful thinking.[59] Certainly, optimism should not be confused with a *false* optimism, which can be dangerous, especially in past and current hot spots like the Middle East. "There is a thin line between hope and delusion, between hope and self-distraction," cautions a contemporary rabbi, Rabbi Michael Marmur, in his 2013 article "The Future of an Illusion."[60] On the other hand, as the Shalom Hartman Institute's Tal Becker writes in his article, "How to be an Optimist in the Middle East:" '[T]he Jewish story... has never been about arriving at the ultimate destination...; it is about recognizing our capacity to move, however incrementally, in the right direction.'[61]

But when you see the green light, the contemporary psychoanalyst and interpreter of biblical and rabbinic literature, Aviva Zornberg, comments, you don't hesitate; you step on the gas and go, you "act on the *basis* of hope."[62]

So in this book, stepping on the gas as I move through 2023, I am still asking this question: What does hope mean in this decade? What does it mean NOW? What does hope mean for the world we presently inhabit? And inherit. What does it mean for its people—us?

I take what the late Rabbi David Hartman wrote about hope in the Jewish tradition as my own mantra: *"The halakhah [the body of Jewish law] does not admit spiritual incapacity….[Hope] says that tomorrow can be better than today."*[63]

Of course, there are many other contemporary points of view (some of which we'll discuss in the next chapters) that demonstrate the very considerable range of current Jewish thought that, in part, deals with the theme of "hope." The diversity of contemporary views on this subject is certainly reflective of the different, often competing, streams of Jewish life today, a situation that prevailed in the early centuries after the destruction of the Second Temple as well. What unifies these views, however, from religious to secular, in the Diaspora and in Israel, is this common understanding: Hope, that vital ingredient of life, initially enshrined in the Psalms and later encoded in the Talmud to keep it safe for future generations, has helped the Jewish people to survive, wherever they found themselves, through the centuries. Key to the understanding of hope in all these references may be summed up once again in the words of Rabbi Bradley Shavit Artson: "And we, an ancient, broken people, we have journeyed on our way across the millennia bringing a message of hope to a broken planet. Do not despair, do not surrender, do not stop."[64]

As a rabbi, I believe that I am in the profession of hope, of comfort, of inspiration—and of action, now mostly through the written word at my advanced age. I believe that the very act of hoping is a *mitzvah*, and many Jewish scholars believe the traditional view that hope leads to redemption.

The Pairing of Hope and Redemption[65]

The late Rabbi David Hartman identifies hope with two essential elements linked to redemption: "the courage to bear human responsibility, to persevere in partial solutions...within contexts of uncertainty [implying no need for utopian goals]...and the expectancy of a future resolution to all human problems."[66]

In addition, the *halakhic* form of hope spurs human action. It's essential, of course, to remember that repentance and good deeds also matter. As does *teshuva*, which involves the fulfilment of three requirements: repentance, restitution, and refraining from repeating the offence in similar circumstances.

In this regard, Hartman cites a Talmudic discussion between two Amoraic teachers, Rav and Shmuel,[67] connecting redemption to repentance and good deeds. Their discussion raises serious questions:[68]

1. Is redemption dependent fully on human choice and man's will to change?

2. Does God enter the process of history by creating conditions compelling people to *teshuva*?

3. Is it possible to construct a viable religious approach without the certainty of redemption?

A single, if ambiguous, answer to all of them exists: Redemption is contingent on human actions. In other words, redemption is importantly connected to hope: We are not trapped in the present but may move forward![69]

Hartman also goes on at length to discuss the views of Maimonides, Nachmanides, the *Mishnah Torah*, Isaiah, and Jeremiah. Essential to Maimonides, for example, is the belief that human beings can always do *teshuvah*. We can change![70] (Certainly, in this century, the slogan, "Yes, we can!" captured the popular imagination in President Obama's presidential campaign.)

Fortunately, Hartman's sense of time is not strictly linear. For him, hope is "a category of transcendence...that opens the present to the future."[71] But it is not merely an expectancy. Two perspectives of time come into it, both the hope for the future and the memory of the past.

As I re-read these words soon after the widely televised January 6th Congressional hearings into the brutal attack on the U.S. Capitol Building took place in 2022, I realized that we may ask other questions:

1. What kind of a future is informed by the past?

2. What lessons do we learn from the present?

3. Can we imagine a positive future, one informed by both past and present, and our own values?

4. What do YOU believe?

CHAPTER 5

WHAT DO YOU BELIEVE?

Why Do We Hope? Some Contemporary Views[72]

There are so many Jewish perspectives on hope, from the Bible to the present day. The selection of contemporary views summarized here all speak to me personally:

1. Rabbi Bradley Shavit Artson's concept of "process thought," the act of "becoming," which I personally endorse.
2. The psychoanalytic perspective of Aviva Gottlieb Zornberg, who links hope and despair.
3. The darker views of David R. Blumenthal, who emphasizes protest, empowerment, and community building, as well as persistence, as a four-fold means to regaining hope. He also believes that the Jews of America and those of Israel have to *share* their hopes for the future of the Jewish people.
4. The raging thoughts of novelist Elie Wiesel, who suggests that remembrance is the key to hope.
5. Hope seen as a miracle, to which I have a strong emotional connection.
6. The historical approach of Rabbi Irving Greenberg, culminating with the establishment of the State of Israel.
7. Eugene B. Borowitz' discussion of secularization's effect on the decline of the Talmud's influence in modern times.[73]
8. Rabbi David Hartman's thoughtful pairing of hope with redemption.

A Psychoanalytic Perspective (or Spiritual Psychology)

In recent decades, it has become popular to combine psychology with theology, at times adding in a little mysticism: all together they comprise a form of spiritual psychology. Foremost among the proponents of this approach is Aviva Gottlieb Zornberg,[74] a top-ranking psychoanalyst and literary scholar in her own right.

In her acclaimed book, *The Beginnings of Desire*, she examines the phenomenon of hope from a psychoanalytic perspective.[75] In Zornberg's view, hope is the other side of brokenness, of despair, so that the two exist in "a kind of twilight zone,"[76] a neither here nor there kind of place. By this she means that people need to go through a state of brokenness to truly get to a state of hope. However, these two extremes do not necessarily exist in sequential or historical order (like plenty followed by famine); sometimes the reverse occurs (famine followed by plenty); at times, the two emotional states are almost simultaneous. When wholeness and security fall apart, she claims, that's when "the opportunity for hope [*sever*] arises," even though hope was irrelevant before the crisis. Hope, for Zornberg, "is *immediately* related to the idea of shattering, of crisis."[77] People often feel alone in their anguish, as my poem, *Alone*, written so long ago at a difficult time, expresses. They feel shattered.

ALONE[8]

The dimming day singed

through fading color patches,

roughed berries dotting rotted piles,

leaves curled tight to cover

death disturbed yet loudly living

huddled in a roaring crowd.

   —Corinne Copnick

Still, I wonder: Is catastrophe necessarily the other side of hope? Surely people can hope for a continuity of a good situation or a bright future, without necessarily suffering, perhaps enduring—catastrophic events. We need to understand, though, that bad things can happen to good people (what Rabbi Harold Kushner wrote about, and so many people read),[79] and not to take good fortune—which can reverse itself in an instant—for granted. And I believe that hope is often related to gratitude. Zornberg does admit that to hope is "to respond with a kind of courage to the surfaces of reality."[80]

A Spectrum of Dynamics

Although Rabbi Professor David R. Blumenthal also connects hope to despair as two sides of the theological coin, he is not as persuaded as Zornberg in this linking; he considers the darker emotions to be stronger than more uplifting ones. Blumenthal's antidote to these dark thoughts is three-fold: "protest, empowerment, and community building, all of which are hopeful because they lead to change—and eventually to a sense of connection to God."[81] And persistence, he claims, is an essential dynamic of hope.

Yet this claim raises some questions for me: Can a person – or a community, or a nation—be persistent if hopelessness is the pervading sentiment? In my view, there must be some remnant of hope to drive the persistence. In other words, persistence falls on the spectrum between hope and despair. Persistence is one of the *tools* needed to move from one pole to the other, provided hope exists.

Blumenthal believes many American Jews hold views that fall into the category of "theological despair...accompanied by underlying rage,"[82] and he offers a diagnosis.

For many American Jews, he claims, this despair is rooted in their indifference and apathy to being Jewish and to Israel. It is similarly connected to growing intermarriage—and, in both America and in Israel, it is rooted in secularism. Blumenthal wonders whether religion or secularism provides a better basis for hope. I wonder if there is an answer to this question, but he implies that both America and Israel must *share* the hope for the future of Judaism (and, I would add, of America). Perhaps that is indeed the answer.

What Do You Believe?

1. Is catastrophe necessarily the other side of hope?

2. Is optimism the same as hope? Is it possible for an individual to hope alone—against all odds?

3. Do you believe that a sense of purpose keeps people alive?

4. To what extent do we change ourselves, and to what extent do we count on helping hands from others?

5. Is it by God's miracles that the people of Israel live? Is rational thinking also an essential tool in moving from despair to hope?

6. What is most effective in inspiring and maintaining hope: Collective Support or Inner Strength?

Collective Support or Inner Strength

So now we come to the all-important question of what is most effective in inspiring and maintaining hope: Is it Collective Support or Inner Strength or both? While it is certainly comforting to have the support of others, is it not possible for an individual to hope—alone—against all odds?

Consider the biblical "Job, our ancestor, our contemporary," as famed novelist Elie Wiesel phrased it.[83] Job lost everything he valued in life yet found the strength to begin again. As one of God's creatures, Job was determined not to repudiate the creation that God had entrusted to him. Instead Job "demonstrated that faith is essential to rebellion, and that hope is possible beyond despair." For both Job and Wiesel, the source of his hope was memory. "Because I remember, I despair," Wiesel wrote. "Because I remember, I...reject despair." [84]

Is hope truly connected, then, to the memory of God's creation, to faith? Where indeed does the biblical Job find his hope? He finds the advice of his friends is useless, and the biblical narrator agrees. God's magnificent speech from the whirlwind only minimizes Job's status as a human being, although it fills him with awe. Finally, he realizes that he can only depend on finding and cultivating his inner strength; that is, he finds his resources for hope within himself.[85]

Consider the pragmatic Rabbi Yohanan. (He saw fighting Rome as suicidal and a dead end.) So he had himself smuggled out of a besieged Jerusalem in a coffin (or so the legend goes) to confront a Roman general, Vespasian, and, in the face of destruction, his courageous action—his *chutzpah*, one might say—ultimately established a new locale for outstanding Torah study in Yavneh.

Consider the thought process of someone like psychiatrist and author Victor Frankl,[86] who emerged from the *Shoah* with hope in his heart and went on to help many people overcome their terrors. Frankl survived four Nazi death camps, including Auschwitz, but lost most of his family in World War II. Yet he was able to teach others, through his famous book, *Man's Search for Meaning* and through his counseling work, about spiritual survival. He called his theory *logotherapy*, from the Greek word *logos* ("meaning"). For Frankl it is not pursuit of pleasure but rather the discovery of what holds personal meaning for us that matters. "Frankl argues that we cannot avoid suffering but we can choose how to cope with it, find meaning in it, and move forward with renewed purpose."[87] A sense of purpose, he believed, keeps people alive. He died in 1997, half a century after the Holocaust.

And consider the pious Jews who wrote questions to Rabbi Ephraim Oshry during their internment in the Kovno ghetto or in concentration camps during WW II, requests he famously buried in cans and published after the war was over. These queries concerned how the internees could live ethically and morally as religious Jews, individually true to the *mitzvoth* in the midst of conditions that degraded them below the level of animals.[88]

I learned about Rabbi Oshry's *Responsa* from Rabbi Daniel Bouskila, one of my distinguished teachers at AJRCA. Rabbi Oshry was considered to be a *poseq*, a scholarly rabbi with great knowledge and experience, a rabbi who knew the Jewish literature intimately and could answer people's questions dealing with the moral and ethical areas of life. He could exercise sensitivity, compassion, creativity, and innovation in his answers—his

Responsa—while remaining true to *halakhic* perspectives. Oshry's view of the *halakha* was tempered by the situation and the need.

What Do You Believe?

Do you believe that:

1. Human beings and the world we inhabit are in a continual state of becoming?
2. The possibility for change is always possible?
3. We change ourselves to some extent but also to some extent count on helping hands from others?
4. Both courage and persistence play a role in maintaining hope?
5. America and Israel need to *share* their hopes for the future of Judaism?
6. We have to be brave enough to dream—and to ACT on those dreams, sometimes against all the odds?
7. That our actions depend on the situation and the need?

CHAPTER 6

HANNAH'S DOUBLE LIFE: THE SITUATION AND THE NEED

"One only loves God with the knowledge with which one

knows him.

According to the knowledge will be the love."

—Moses Maimonides[89]

*D*uring the Holocaust, Rabbi Ephraim Oshry—known to be a deeply compassionate scholar of Jewish law—was considered the spiritual leader of the Kovno ghetto. In this role, he tried to help the members of this community, subjected to horrific conditions, to maintain a semblance of Jewish life. He endeavored to answer many difficult questions of Jewish law for the troubled ghetto Jews. Oshry's genius was his creative ability to find a way to say "yes" instead of a blanket "no."[90]

But this is not a story about Rabbi Oshry's genius. It is the story of my friend, Hannah (not her real name), who was still bedeviled by her Jewish identity at the late age of 82. Like the many people who wrote to Rabbi Oshry during and after WWII, individuals trying their best to live up to the standards of Jewish law—to remain good human beings in the eyes of God despite their behavior in appalling circumstances—I am asking a question on behalf of Hannah's soul as, unknowingly, she prepares to meet her Maker.[91]

Hannah was spared the horrors of Hitler's Germany by the actions of her father in gaining a Christian identity, intended to protect her from anticipated harm. Yet caught in a web of ambivalence, she was not spared the suffering of her soul. So here is the question (the *she'ela*)—the many questions, in fact—that, as a rabbi, I am asking for her because she cannot ask them for herself. Perhaps there is no answer.

The Questions:

1. Can someone born into Judaism, but forced into Catholicism from early teen years, by parents anxious to protect her, return to Judaism on a part-time basis?
2. Can she go back and forth between the two religions—and their two communities—and still be considered a Jew?
3. Can she still be a Jew if she marries a Catholic and brings up her children as Catholics—even though she is no longer a practicing Catholic herself?
4. Is she a Jew or a Christian if she is involved in leadership positions in the Jewish community?
5. Is she a Jew or a Christian if she reverts to Catholicism for fear of losing her soul and going to eternal hell fire as the approach of the end of life draws near?

The Back Story:

Hannah was born into a wealthy, educated, and cultured Jewish family in Holland (her father was a diamond dealer). She remembered that they lived as Jews and had Jewish friends. But as Hitler came to power in Germany and began to make aggressive moves against the Jewish communities, her father realized that the Dutch Jews would soon be in danger in Holland (where there were already rumblings against the Jews), and he began to make plans to protect his family. Since his livelihood was a portable one, he took his wife and three young daughters to Paris, where, far from their usual associations, they submerged themselves in a secular world. They hurriedly studied French while he made the necessary arrangements to take them to Montreal in Quebec, Canada, but both parents were aware that they still counted as Jews (even if they claimed they were secular), rapidly being characterized by Nazi elements as the vermin of Europe.

It was toward the end of 1938 when they finally arrived in Montreal. As the news from Europe grew worse (Canada entered the war in 1939, well before the U.S. did), Hannah's father quickly took his three daughters to a Montreal convent with beautiful facilities and excellent educational reputation in Montreal. At the time, neither this city's Catholic majority nor its Anglo minority could be considered fond of Jews, but although slurs against Jews certainly occurred on the part of individuals in this time of economic depression, there was no official antisemitism, as there was in many parts of Europe. Hannah's father instructed the nuns to educate his blonde, blue-eyed girls as Catholics. In the event that

Hitler's reach would (God forbid!) extend to Canada, he made a gift of a considerable sum of money to the convent. "If anything happens, protect my children," he beseeched them. That is how it happened that Hannah, born a Jew, was educated to be a Catholic. At this early age—she was fourteen and still a minor following her parent's bidding—she did not understand all her father's reasoning, but she came to truly love the pageantry and rituals of the Catholic service, particularly Mass, and was intrigued by the lives of the Saints.

She dimly remembered that her parents continued to have Jewish friends and to live their lives, although largely secular, as Jewish people. Protected by the convent, however, the three daughters were trained to be Catholics. Later in life, two of the daughters, younger than Hannah, refused to admit that they had ever been Jewish, born of Jewish parents. But Hannah knew.

After the war, she was educated at the Sorbonne in Paris, and her Francophile identity was both reinforced and welcomed when she returned to Montreal. She did not have an identity problem then; she was a French-speaking Catholic. *Point final.* She sang Canada's national anthem (with Quebec nationalistic fervor) in French. With her love of Catholic pageantry, she was attracted to the theatre, where she met the charismatic actor who was to become her husband. He was Catholic, and in due course, they had two children, both brought up as Catholics.

Eventually Hollywood's artistic top echelon called on her husband's talents, and that's where her identity problem resurfaced. In Los Angeles, far from the circles she frequented in Montreal, Hannah was drawn to the Jewish community, and, as time went on, involved in its leadership. Then, as her children grew and moved back to Montreal, she became increasingly active in the L.A. Jewish community and contributed generously to many Jewish charities.

However, she never attended synagogue services. Never. Nor, as a non-practicing Catholic, did she attend Catholic, or indeed, any kind of religious services. She was vocal, though, against Israel's "policies," and thus relieved her guilt and ambivalence towards her Jewish antecedence by her attitude towards Israel (which she eventually visited with a church group). But, despite her anti-religious, anti-Israel posture, there was no doubt about it: she was magnetically drawn to the Jewish community. It was there that she felt most at home.

Yet there was another side to the coin. Whenever she returned to Montreal for a visit with her children and friends, she immediately reverted to her French Catholic past life and associations, although she did not attend Catholic services there either. But she always felt guilty—wherever she was. She felt guilty in Montreal because she was hiding her Jewishness, and she felt guilty in Los Angeles because she was hiding her Catholicism.

A Double Life:

When I met Hannah in Los Angeles some twenty years ago, she was a widow. No more Catholic husband to complicate things. Her children were far away. I assumed that she was Jewish because of her activities in Jewish organizations, but, as our friendship grew, she confided to me how tortured she felt about her identity.

"I feel like such a hypocrite," she said. "When I am in Los Angeles, I lead a Jewish life. I have Jewish friends. I belong—and lead—Jewish organizations. But when I am in Montreal with my children and grandchildren, I live as a Catholic."

She was leading a double life—a tale of two religions, two cultures—in terms of her identity, yet she denied being "religious." She was secular, she would insist. So her religious orientation didn't matter. Nor she did follow Jewish religious practice in secret, as the *Marranos* (victims of the Spanish inquisition in the late 1400s and 1500s) once did.

"There are many paths to God, "I would suggest, not as a rabbi but as a friend. "For you, there was a fork in the road, and the path you took was chosen for you by someone else. Since you travel both paths, why not enjoy the best of each of them and learn from them. But you know, Hannah, eventually you will have to decide for yourself, to make a choice."

Still, as she grew older, Hannah became increasingly uneasy about her identity, secular though she proclaimed it to be.

"Sometimes I miss the rituals and pageantry of the Catholic Mass," she would say wistfully. "Sometimes I dream about them. My grandchildren are Catholic." Yet she still resisted going to services of any kind. Not Jewish, not Catholic.

When she decided to move from her apartment to an Assisted Living facility, she gave away many of her possessions to charitable organizations, and she also gave some lovely things to her children and friends, including me. Wanting to reciprocate, I thought long and hard before I decided what I could give to her in return, something small that she could take with her to her new home. She already had everything material anyone could want. What didn't she have? Peace of mind. To what degree can we accept uncertainty? How do we handle these tensions?

When I lived in Canada, I owned an art and antique gallery for a number of years, and among the antique jewelry I had retained when I closed the gallery was a beautiful, large, antique cross, dating from the 1850s. Silver on gold (as was often done in those days) and ornamented with little diamonds, it hung from a silver chain.

I had already donated the Jewish ritual items I owned to a local Judaica museum, but the curator didn't want the cross. Now, many years later, I decided to gift it to Hannah, who was already well settled in the Assisted Living facility but still breathing at night with the help of an oxygen tank. "This is for you Hannah," I said.

"Your father wanted you to be protected. When you wear it, you'll be doing what your father wanted."

"There is always antisemitism," she replied, tears welling up in her eyes. "It never goes away." Immediately, she put the cross around her neck and smiled joyfully. She has been wearing it *underneath* her clothing ever since.

"Now you have decided for yourself," I said. "There is comfort in that. God's world is for everyone."

With a failing heart, in fear, she had chosen her path, like the hidden Jews who still live in New Mexico and elsewhere as Catholics, secreting their true Jewish identity 500 years after the Spanish Inquisition in fear of a persecution-to-come. But in Hannah's case, it was a cross, not a Jewish star, that she wore under her clothing, next to the heart.

In Hebrew, the word for heart is "*lev.*" The heart's beating is connected to the pulse of our being. And to our minds. The heart always knows.

"What the heart is to the body, the Jewish people are to the world," wrote the famous poet Judah Halevi.[92] It is a heart that has continued beating for thousands of years.

WHO?[93]

Who can dry the tears of God?

Is it the earth forever

quivering with remorse

or space itself curving

to cradle such pain?

Who can share the fears of God?

Is it man and wife grown

old in friendship enfolding

family before and

after their ending?

Who can light the face of God?

Is it an artist's fiery spirit

steeping red-blossomed in

a rose-petal's clear

white water?

Who can feel the touch of God?

Is it our sleeping child

caressing once more

the wounded world

with wakened wonder?

Who can know the mind of God?

Ah!...

—*Corinne Copnick*

CHAPTER 7

LET MY PEOPLE GO: FREE SOVIET JEWRY (1964-1991)

*B*eing alive for so long certainly has its historical advantages. In the 1970s, I was in my thirties, living in a beautiful, spacious cottage in the Town of Mount Royal (a suburb of Montreal) with my husband and our four great kids. I vividly remember the gargantuan 1970s efforts of Western Jews to free Soviet Jews from repression. *Refusniks*! That's what Soviet authorities called Jews who were denied permission to emigrate. The Free Soviet Jewry movement began as an international human rights campaign mainly concentrated in the United States and the Soviet Union. The purpose was largely to raise awareness that Jews were not permitted to emigrate from the Soviet Union.[94]

In short, many established Jewish organizations participated and coordinated their efforts. The American Jewish Committee and the World Jewish Congress joined forces in the newly named National Conference on Soviet Jewry (NCJS). Student organizations got involved too. For years, there were many demonstrations and activities in aid of these goals. [95]

Throughout, these efforts centered on diplomacy and protesting peacefully as a means to create public awareness of the need for Soviet-persecuted Jews and others to be allowed to emigrate to other countries, specifically Israel, and the U.S. Behind the scenes meetings also took place.[96]

I remember the "Save Soviet Jewry" movement in Canada, as far more passionate than the above factual description of the

Soviet Jewry movement, gleaned partly from *Wikipedia*, partly from my own recollection. What added drive and personal identification to the movement, was the courage, this essential component of hope, of individuals—and, in particular of Natan Sharansky,[97] whose dire situation became the public face of the movement. Sharansky was imprisoned for refusing to submit to a totalitarian regime in the hope of a better future. During the Cold War, he was known widely as a Soviet *refusnik*, imprisoned for his oppositional stands. After his release from prison, he resettled in Israel, continuing his work as a human rights activist, and eventually an Israeli politician, and an author, whose opinions are esteemed in the Western world.[98]

Although *Miracles Are What You Make of Them* does not deal specifically with the *Shoah*, or with the inhumanities of totalitarian systems that attempt to destroy the human spirit, a discussion of hope—or *the miraculous sustenance of hope*—would not be complete without mentioning them here. Sadly, we see such inhumanities every day now on our television or computer screens or phones.

One might ask what sort of theology or anthropology would presume to have hope after the *Shoah?*[99] Or after what is happening now? But maybe that kind of inextinguishable hope and the capacity to sustain it nevertheless—and act on it— *is* a miracle.

* * * *

Historically Speaking

There is, of course, an historical approach to hope, one that can be shaped in many ways. For example, Rabbi Irving Greenberg's views have been markedly influenced by the Holocaust of World War II. Perhaps that is why he teaches that historical thinking is a useful tool in moving from despair to hope.[100] While the Holocaust has been a defining moment for Jewish people in the 20th century, there have been many other catastrophes of great significance to Jewish history, such as the exile to Babylon, the destruction of the Second Temple in Jerusalem, the *Bar Kochba* Revolt, the Inquisition, resulting in the expulsion of Jews from Spain and other countries, pogroms in Europe and elsewhere.

Even in this 21st century, genocidal behavior recurs in our world, such as threats of genocide and terror attacks from Islamic actors and now once again devastating Russian aggression, not in Chechnya this time but in Ukraine, all of which bring with them memories of many other persecutions of Jews throughout our history. As with the biblical Amalek, we are cautioned to remember not to forget. With contemporary school shootings and increasingly frequent antisemitic acts and hostile comments, especially on social media, it's getting easier and easier to remember. Certainly, from our own history, Jewish people have learned the hard way that many little events can replicate and grow into movements and— unless serious attention is paid to the development of this process—they can morph into big events that are eventually disastrous for Jews who historically become the scapegoats. (I shudder to remember that my birth sign is Capricorn, the goat.)

Fortunately, Rabbi Greenberg keeps his historical calm despite the growing chaos in the world. There is an evolving process within Judaism, he explains, with the Holocaust marking the third of its three stages: the biblical period (which ended with the destruction of the two Temples); the rabbinic period (which ended with the Holocaust); and the Holocaust and its aftermath, culminating with the establishment of the State of Israel.

In the biblical period, Greenberg reminds us, God was the sole redeemer, and therefore the covenant was an unequal contract. However, in the rabbinic period, God no longer intervened in history. In response, the rabbis reinterpreted the covenant (the Oral Torah), which eventually morphed into the Written Torah, to give humans more initiative and responsibility. Then the Holocaust (the *Shoah*) created a new paradigm in which redemption took a back seat to human efforts, with God acting through those efforts.

The Holocaust led to "a heightened tension between faith and doubt, hope and despair, triumph of life and victory of death," declares Rabbi Greenberg.[101] In fact, the only response to the Holocaust is to affirm life,[102] and "only the hope engendered by the 'miraculous' deliverance of Israel during the Six-Day War allowed

Jews to face the full horror of the Holocaust."[103] Yes, a miracle. For Greenberg, the dream is still alive.

Although Eugene B. Borowitz also takes an historical approach to hope's relationship to the evolution of Judaism, his opinion is quite different from the views expressed by Rabbi Greenberg. In Borowitz' article, "Hope Jewish and Hope Secular,"[104] he echoes Greenberg's assertion that the reestablishment of Israel enabled Jewish people to hope once again (that is, Redemption became equated with the State of Israel.) However, he believes that it impossible to talk about hope today without taking into account the continual state of Arab-Israeli conflict in Israel: "Jewish hope...is linked to what God does in historic time...and in our times that means, among other communities, quite specifically the State of Israel."[105]

In other words, for Borowitz, hope is focused neither on the World-to-Come nor on some imaginary world disconnected from the reality of this world. Sometimes the reality can be overwhelming.

I recently read an extraordinary book by Dara Horn, who is well connected to the real world as she shares biblical, Talmudic, and contemporary knowledge. Small wonder that her book has earned high critical praise and several prestigious literary awards. Although the title, *People Love Dead Jews: Reports from a Haunted Present,* may shock you, the author is determined to show it's true.

For a public desensitized by the media, increasing antisemitic incidents at universities, public events, or poisonous hatred on the Internet can't compete with the horrific, large-scale cruelty of the *Shoah*. "The Holocaust happened," she suggests, "because entire societies abdicated responsibility for their own problems, and instead blamed them on the people who represented...the thing they were most afraid of: responsibility."[106]

It is not by chance that the national anthem of Israel is called *Hatikvah* ("The Hope").

Rabbi Greenberg is much more optimistic. Yes, he fervently believes, there will likely be another miracle, a fourth stage to the evolution of Judaism: the extension of the covenant to all people. And I hope with all my heart that, despite all the ugly happenings that occur from time to time in this world, despite all the horrible news in the newspapers I read daily online, this fourth stage will eventually come into being. *Not yet*, as the rabbis remind us. But maybe sooner than we think. Yes, Rabbi Greenberg, I believe in miracles.

UNITY[107]

Loving

people

for us

are

separate

forms

sharing

common

energy

uncommonly.

—*Corinne Copnick*

CHAPTER 8
TWO MIRACLES

AKHNAI'S OVEN
THE HEREM OF ANONY-MOUS

$\mathcal{S}$ ome Talmudic stories deal with the insidious effect that evil speech can have on a society, and how the repeated expression of lies against an individual can become a rapidly spreading "group think" that can take down even a previously highly placed and well-respected individual. In the Jewish tradition, it is called *lashon hara*—an evil tongue. In the contemporary vernacular, we usually call it gossip, which may sometimes be harmless and often finds a receptive audience. Unfortunately, sometimes the gossipers have ulterior motives and can damage the reputation of the person or persons who are targeted by the *lashon hara*.

A well-known Hasidic folk tale about gossip getting out of hand in is often told by rabbis to demonstrate the harm that *lashon hara* can do, and the difficulty in taking back the resultant damage, even if unintentional, caused by "evil tongues." Contemporary rabbis often repeat the following simple parable. Its main feature is a pillow full of feathers.

This folktale explains that even if the gossip is repeated by the teller to only one person "in confidence," that person may inadvertently (or sometimes deliberately) tell another person, and this pattern is repeated over and over again until damage is done to a person's reputation in the community. In current times, when the dimension of far-reaching social media comes into play, the damage may be irreparable.

So what can illustrate this process better than a pillow full of feathers? To paraphrase the long-ago story, gleaned from Eastern Europe. On a windy day, the rabbi calls in the perpetrator of some ugly gossip that has consumed the congregation and asks the person to please bring a feather pillow to their meeting. Then the rabbi instructs the gossiper to slit the pillowcase and throw feathers all over his study. The congregant is shocked. "What a mess!" he cries. Then the rabbi, opening the study's window, tells the congregant to release the feathers to the breezy air, which of course, blows them all over the place.

"Oops!" exclaims the rabbi, "we need those feathers back! What good is a pillow without its feathers? Go and gather them all back right away, every single one."

"But it's impossible," the dismayed congregant replies. "I can't retrieve them. They have flown all over the place. They're everywhere."

"Ah," says the rabbi. "Just imagine how gossipy stories or rumors can take wing. Once your words are out of your mouth, you can't get them back."

Hurtful words—the evil tongue—and, even worse, the "group think" that may result from their dissemination—can indeed do a lot of damage, as the Talmudic narrative of "Akhnai's Oven" demonstrates. It was written long before there was an Internet. In fact, the Talmud equates the public harming of a person's reputation to be equivalent to murder. In contemporary times, we call it defamation. With this said, here is my take on "Akhnai's Oven."

* * * *

Akhnai's Oven

The narrative of *Akhnai's Oven* employs many of the literary characteristics of Talmudic stories.[108] Among them, it has a cast made up of rabbis. As Rabbi Vizotsky notes in *Sage Tales*,[109] the stories introduce a cast of rabbinic characters that become increasingly familiar as the narrative dramas unfold, much like actors in a weekly television drama (*Breaking Bad*, for example) with overtones that become more and more serious as the show continues.

The esteemed rabbis who are the actors in this story are all members of the *Sanhedrin*, and they are deliberating in a lawyerly way in the House of Study. Prominent among them is Rabbi Eliezer, whom, we are told, is usually correct when it comes to matters of Jewish law, of *halakhah*. And remember, it's the majority decision that becomes Jewish law.

* * * *

Loving Disputes

The rabbis of the Talmud believed that in order to understand a situation fully, and to make a decisive resolution (where possible), it was best to take all aspects of a situation into consideration. This entailed different points of view, and they were able to hold multiple points of view in their minds as true, each from their own perspective. The Talmudic method was one that fostered a delight in argumentation, but they were intended as loving disputes. Of course, eventually they had to come to a decision, and then the majority decision ruled. But the minority decision was also recorded (because times change, and different decisions may be needed). Interestingly, the U.S. justice system has many similarities to Jewish law, especially in terms of the way appeals and the Supreme Court work.

The Talmudic tale of *"Akhnai's Oven"* (a circuitous story that begins with loving disputes about repairing and purifying a broken oven and, unfortunately, takes a long and not so loving route to its resolution) is one of these disputes.

Now Rabbi Eliezer is usually a very persuasive sage, used to being Number One rabbi, but as the story proceeds, we get the feeling that the other rabbis are jealous of him. Their words encircle him like snakes.

What the rabbis are debating about is Akhnai's oven. Akhnai is the person who owns the oven, which has been dismantled because it was ritually impure, and put together again in sections with sand cemented in between them. Now this group of rabbis is discussing whether or not Akhnai's oven can be ritually pure if the section that was previously contaminated does not touch any other section. Thus the oven could still be used.

So the story begins as a folk tale that does not seem to be about such a serious issue. But the full story is told, Talmud-style in a complex, round-about way. So the story begins simply, but then it escalates. By the latter part of this metaphorical Talmudic tale, the audience learns that it really concerns the defamation and mistreatment of that brilliant individual, Rabbi Eliezer, by a rabbinic majority (the rest of the rabbis) who oppose his views:

Rabbi Eliezer thinks it would be permissible for Akhnai to use his put-together oven. The other rabbis do not. So, when his words fail to persuade them, the story brings the literary device of magical events into play to prove the point. (It is reminiscent of the biblical scene where Moses tries to persuade Pharaoh of the power of God through magic tricks.)

First Rabbi Eliezer (whose efforts are intended to demonstrate that God agrees with his position, and therefore he is not doing magic) announces that, to demonstrate that his opinion reflects Divine Will, the nearby carob tree will move; it will uproot and then re-root itself a short distance away. The carob tree obeys Rabbi Eliezer's command, but the rabbis are unimpressed. A carob tree cannot decide matters, they say. Their answer is the same when Rabbi Eliezer commands a body of water to reverse its direction, and the body of water does so. Then Rabbi Eliezer commands the walls of the House of Study to lean in, but, as a compromise and mark of respect to the other rabbis too, the walls only lean in half-way, like the leaning Tower of Pisa.

Finally, in exasperation at the rabbi's intransigence, a Divine voice calls from heaven—a *bat kol* (which literally means "daughter of the Voice," often translated as a "Divine Echo)—to support Rabbi Eliezer's decision. But the other rabbis are unconvinced. "It [the Torah] is not in heaven!" they declare. What they mean is that God has empowered learned sages to articulate Torah in its fullest sense, and therefore the Divine Voice, the *bat kol*, should not interfere in earthly matters. So the concept of hope is already embedded in the story through free will and social processes of decision-making. Human beings have the ability to make their own decisions to effect change—for good or bad.

Unfortunately, after Rabbi Eliezer leaves the meeting in disgust, the other rabbis are vindictive toward him. He throws his weight around too much, they grumble. Even though heaven itself supported his opinion, it is the minority opinion, and they are the majority, and even though Rabbi Eliezer is right, the majority opinion will hold. Even if the decision is wrong, the process is right. At least from God's perspective, God has also validated the procedural rule of majority vote.

When God hears that the rabbis will not listen to the Divine Voice from heaven, he chuckles, and he exclaims, "My sons have defeated me, my sons have defeated me." Is God proud, the way parents are proud when children surpass them, or is the laughter of the Divine foreshadowing something punitive? By the time the story ends, God will have the last laugh.

But the group of rabbis do not know this yet. Feeling triumphant, the jealous rabbis go even further. In spite, they decide to excommunicate Rabbi Eliezer, to banish him from the community. The Talmud doesn't pull any punches as it tackles the anguish that a group can inflict to magnify the pain.

Their action is called a *herem*, and it means that no one in the community will talk to him; they will not have anything to do with him; he is excommunicated. Rabbi Eliezer, who has already been defamed by malicious words, is now hurt by the *withdrawal of words*.[110] The rabbis send Rabbi Eliezer's good friend, Rabbi Akiva, to inform him of their cruel decision.

What is remarkable is the delicate tact with which Rabbi Akiva communicates to Rabbi Eliezer the *herem* that has been pronounced on him. He dresses in black, as if he were in mourning, because Rabbi Eliezer is now as if dead to the community, and when he enters the house, he sits quietly until Rabbi Eliezer addresses him. And when Rabbi Akiva informs him of the decision, tears fill Rabbi Eliezer's eyes. It is Rabbi Akiva's gentle words and actions that, to this day, influence Jewish behavior on entering a house of mourning. Of course, Eliezer already understood what had transpired, and what his status was from Akiva's actions.

But that night nature takes its revenge. The laughter of the Divine is indeed double-edged. While God, the parent, laughs indulgently at the *chutzpah* of his Children who reject the interference of heaven in earthly matters, God also shows that the power of the Divine still reigns supreme. While the rabbis who excommunicated Rabbi Eliezer exult in the supremacy of human rationality, there are Divine consequences to the evil words of the rabbis, and to the pain caused to Rabbi Eliezer by the pronouncement of the *herem* and the withholding of their words. First God punishes them for this audacity through Rabbi Eliezer who burns the crops and, it is said, makes the dough swell in women's hands. Then God wreaks vengeance on these upstart rabbis through the power of nature.

The heavens rage, and the seas storm. Rabbi Gamliel, the brother of Rabbi Eliezer's wife and President of the Sanhedrin, who supported the other rabbis' decisions from afar, is caught in the stormy sea. And even though Rabbi Eliezer's wife, ironically named *Imma Shalom*, the Mother of Peace, tries to prevent Rabbi Eliezer from prostrating himself in prayer because she does not want his tears to reach the gates of heaven—where she realizes God will take pity on him and enact further revenge on the perpetrators and on her brother, Rabbi Gamliel—and result in her own brother's death.

Despite *Imma Shalom's* precautions, Rabbi Eliezer's tears *do* reach the gates of heaven, and they open wide for him because he has been painfully wounded by *ona'at devarim* (inflicting pain on someone with hurtful words). Furthermore, God not only strikes down Rabbi Gamliel, but also nature continues to rage against the community. For much of the story, it seems as if all hope has been lost for Rabbi Eliezer, and, as if the story ends with a this-worldly resolution and death. Yet, at the end, hope not only returns, but it also assumes eschatological significance. The Talmud tells us that, even though the gates to heaven have been locked since the destruction of the Second Temple, they open to the tears of those who have been cruelly wounded by *ona'at devarim,* by the pain inflicted by words. This is a powerful message of both hope for the victims and a warning to the oppressors.

This story, remember, started with a controversy about the purity of a broken oven and then led to the brokenness caused to an individual. Can a person wounded by evil gossip also be put back together—that is, be whole—again? That is the question the story is really asking. Thankfully, towards the end of the tale, there is a hopeful answer: The pained tears of broken Rabbi Eliezer, wounded by words, gain him redemption—and entrance to the World-to-Come.

The *Herem* of Anony-Mous

I was so intrigued by the story of Ahknai's Oven that I subsequently cast a real-life encounter with a superb individual into the following narrative, based on elements of the Talmudic story. Inspired by this Talmudic tale, my own narrative, *"The Herem (Banishment) of Anony-Mous,* is a round-about story about wrong, shame, recovery, and a heavenly voice called the *bat kol*.

In *Akhnai's Oven*, the reader or listener does not know where the story is going until it gets there. In the same round-about manner, *The Herem of Anony-Mous* makes the point of the narrative. My story is a contemporary illustration of how any gathering of people with group-think (not necessarily Jewish people), can inflict pain—*ona'ah*—on a talented person with original ideas beyond the capacity of the group to understand. The story makes much use of an oft-used literary device characteristic of rabbinic narratives: the divine voice from heaven (the *bat kol*), while the banishment of Anony-Mous from his community—and his music—parallels the *herem* imposed on the Talmud's Rabbi Eliezer.

A Contemporary Fable: Group Think in Action

Anony-Mous was not Jewish; he lived in remote area of North China where it was unlikely that he would ever encounter a Jew. But Anony-Mous did have a religion of his own, although he didn't know it was a religion. He called it Music. He did not have to seek Music. It came to him, as if he had a Divine Voice, a *bat kol* in his head. The *bat kol* was with him always, when he rose up and when he lay down to sleep. It was always there.

The poor, uneducated people who lived in the rural, impoverished town in North China where he was born didn't have musical training, but Anony-Mous' *bat kol* could transport them to internal places they understood from nature, from the sparse trees in the area, and the waterfall's flow. They understood the sounds of the birds and the animals, and they heard the breath of the wind, the *ru-ach*. But never before had anyone in their town made the beautiful "Music" that came from Anony-Mous' *bat kol*.

On their home-made instruments the villagers tried to reproduce the sounds that Anony-Mous played on his improvised instruments as if truly a Divine Voice were directing him. This was the first miracle, that a little boy could hear that Voice and create its sound for all to hear.

The people whispered about this miracle to the nearby villagers, who whispered to other villagers, and soon the news of Anony-Mous' *bat kol* traveled all the way to Beijing, the capital of China, and the home of its musical culture. The Beijing Opera, for example, was there, along with some of the finest musicians and music teachers in all of China.

Anony-Mous was eight years old when Chinese officials from the capital visited the little town to hear his music and promptly whisked him off to Beijing, where he was housed and fed in a style he had never experienced and given the rigorous training accorded to those whose musical genius came to the attention of the State. This was the second miracle. Anony-Mous' *bat kol* was very happy there and sang in his head all day long and sometimes all night too, as Anony-Mous learned from expert teachers to write down the notes of the Divine Voice in his head. By the time he was twenty, he was composing music—operas, symphonies, concertos—not only in the Chinese style, but in the Western method he was learning too. He was greatly attracted by what he learned about the West, where there was a political system called "democracy," as if all the instruments in the orchestra had a chance to play so that their voices could be heard.

By now Anony-Mous was not only conducting an orchestra, he was also a university student at Beijing's finest facility, where ideas he had never encountered before floated around surreptitiously. Unwisely, he took a leadership role in a student protest: The students wanted the government to ameliorate impoverished conditions throughout China—poverty very unlike the elegant living to which Anony-Mous had been introduced in Beijing. He wanted to make life better for simple people, like those who had valued the soulful beauty of his *bat kol* when he was a little boy. The Chinese government's reaction was harsh: It was dangerous to allow a charismatic leader like Anony-Mous to disrupt society with his Western ideas. Even if the rural people of China were indeed suffering dire poverty while Beijing officials lived in luxury. Even if Anony-Mous was right, and they were wrong. Even if his *bat kol* sang out in magnificent music that celebrated and supported these ideas. The people were listening, and they might begin to understand where the *bat kol* was leading. An individual must bend to the majority decisions.

The majority decision of the Chinese court was dire: *herem*, banishment. The learned judges had the power to execute him if they so decided. Instead, they tried to kill his *bat kol*, his special power that came from a place they could not understand. They realized that it was not Anony-Mous but the magnetism of his *bat kol* that could lead the people astray. So not only did they banish him from the capital and sentence him to hard labor in a remote agricultural commune in North China, but the judges further decreed that he could not write music nor play an instrument. Not for twenty years. Their intention was to break his spirit into defamed pieces, like the sections of Akhnai's oven that were no longer ritually pure. Anony-Mous was made *tamei* (impure).

That night, with uncontrolled anger, the *bat kol* wreaked vengeance on the capitol. The wind howled, uprooting the trees, the waters reversed their direction, and the earth shook, causing the very walls of the courthouse that had witnessed Anony-Mous' sentencing to bend perpetually in penance. The animals screamed in terror. But the people were silent. They understood that their beloved *bat kol* was leaving them.

Miraculously, the *bat kol* did not leave Anony-Mous. That was the third miracle. Like the *Shechina,*[111] it accompanied him to the remote rural community where his muscles would ache from the hard labor and the harsh climate until he got used to it and became very, very strong. Inside and out. Although he was not permitted to sing, play an instrument, or write a note of music, the *bat kol* sang in his head day and night—as he was awakening to the dawn, while he was working throughout the day, and as he was going to sleep. It created beautiful operas and symphonies, and concertos that only Anony-Mous could hear. For nineteen years. In the twentieth year of his harsh sentence, he was permitted to conduct a rural orchestra in the village where the labor camp was located, and where he improvised rough instruments. As the stirring notes of the *bat kol* took heart and emerged in the compositions he created for the orchestra, the people were awed. The notes were not yet written down. They were all in his head.

At the end of the twentieth year, the authorities whisked him back to Beijing as if the *herem* had never happened. He was considered "re-educated" and reinstated to all his former musical glory. Then he was formally introduced to the current female director of the Beijing Opera, whom he married, and they had a son—who perhaps one day, if Anony-Mous is lucky, will surpass him. It was like the restoration of Job after all his hardships. Or the restoration of Akhnai's oven that had been dismembered but put together with sand between the three sections so that it could remain pure.

Yes, there are some pure individuals who must adhere to their own absolute truth, despite the consequences. No matter what happened to Anony-Mous, he had kept faith with the *bat kol*. Finally, his tears at the *ona'ah*, the pain inflicted on an individual by a group, by a majority that was wrong, had penetrated God's gates, even though they remained locked to others. Now, aided by the *bat kol*, the notes emerged from his head and flooded onto pages and pages of musical compositions. As one of the foremost modern composers in China, Anony-Mous would become well known in the West for compositions that reconciled the sounds of Eastern and Western music into a unified whole. And the *bat kol* rejoiced. When Anony-Mous' music is played all over the world, some say they can hear the *bat kol*— or is it God?—laughing.

* * * *

Is this a true story?

Who was my Anony-Mous (not his real name)? Like Rabbi Eliezer, Anony-Mous was cruelly treated by his community. He, too, had suffered the debilitating effects of *ona'ah*, and eventually— twenty years later—his tears penetrated the locked gates too. I encountered him at the Banff Centre for the Arts in Alberta,

Canada, where we were both guest artists in different disciplines and became friends. In his early fifties then, tall for a Chinese man, slim, and fit, with black hair, flashing black eyes, and hands that gesticulated like an impassioned actor captured on film, he was in the process of writing a symphony for presentation at the Lincoln Centre. Although his studio at the Banff Centre was furnished with a grand piano, he rarely used it. The notes of his composition simply poured out of his head to his pen and transferred themselves to paper in astounding fluidity. Cemented together like Akhnai's oven, he was purified. He had emerged from his broken state, from a *herem* that would have broken lesser souls to become the musical pride of China.

Rabbi Corinne Copnick

NEVER SAY GOOD-BYE[112]

Oh Promised Land, where the sky is my friend,

and double rainbows, triumphant,

circle the sun,

where a community of artists

co-create, painting in tongues,

making music with words,

writing in sound, rhythmically

blended in the nestling curve of

mountainous arms...

where memories of craggy rockfaces

etch themselves in my eye's lens,

arch imprints of tomorrow's

vision wherever, transported,

it may be newly invoked...

where I pass from this camera'd,

heady air without leaving because

its eternal fragrance wafts within

me, and the soaring snowpeaks stand,

believing, there.

—*Corinne Copnick*

SECTION THREE

THE DREAM OF THE GENERATIONS

Declaration of Independence of the State of Israel plaque *given to my father, Dr. Irving Copnick, among others, for helping Israel reach this day. The plaque graced the walls of my parents' home for many years, and now it hangs on the walls of the home where I live with my daughter and grandchild. L'dor va dor. From generation to generation. Many young people have not read the Declaration, which is transcribed in Appendix 2. (Photo J. Spiegel, ©Los Angeles, 2023.)*

CHAPTER 9

OPENING THE LETTERS OF MY SOUL

A SPIRITUAL HOME

WHO WAS MORDECAI NOAH?

DELARATION OF INDEPENDENCE

REDEMPTION AND THE STATE OF ISRAEL

*T*he Dream: The island was a land mass, eight miles long and six miles wide, located in the Niagara River near Buffalo. The idea, with the blessing of the State of New York, was to create a temporary homeland for the persecuted Jews of the world under American protection. It was to be called Ararat (symbolizing Noah's Ark, which some believe to be stranded atop Mount Ararat). It was 1820.

Our dreams are pointers to our future. In that sense, we should believe in them. At the age of 72, I had a dream—a dream about becoming a rabbi. It seemed an impossible accomplishment at my age—especially since I had still to learn the Hebrew language (initially just to read and write it)—yet seven years of dedicated study later, I was ordained as a rabbi in Los Angeles.

According to the Sages in the Talmud, "It is an open question as to whether dreams have a validity" (Berachot 55a). But in the same Talmudic section, Rav Hisda tells us that a dream that is not interpreted is like a letter which is not read. Dreams are the unopened letters of the soul. When we have the courage to open them, they point to the paths we need to follow—our soul paths—if only we can find the moral strength to do it. However, dreams, the Talmud cautions, are 1/60th of prophecy. That still gives us 59/60ths to fulfill. It takes a lot of hard work!

A Spiritual Home

Did you ever hear of Mordecai Manuel Noah (a different Noah from the biblical one)? Few people today have. When I first learned about Mordecai Noah's quest, I was so intrigued that I considered making his efforts—and Grand Island in the U.S.—the topic of my rabbinic master's thesis. However, when I explored this theme further, I discovered that a Ph.D. student, Jerry Klinger, had already written a doctoral dissertation about Mordecai Noah, an early American Zionist who filled an American diplomatic Consular post and other activities in the Jacksonian era with great panache. In reading and absorbing Klinger's unpublished Ph.D. thesis: *"Major Noah: American Patriot, American Zionist,"* I learned a great deal about Mordecai Noah's quest and about the dynamic character of Noah himself. Klinger later became the President of the Jewish American Society for Historical Preservation.[113]

I also learned that Cornell University holds many of the fascinating authentic documents relating to Grand Island, Mordecai Noah's projected U.S. place of safety—intended as a temporary refuge—for the persecuted Jews of the world. On March 5, 1886, he read his essay, *"Founding the City of Arafat on Grand Island,"* to an upscale "Society" gathering in Troy, New York. The paper was eventually republished by Cornell University in 1993—107 years later.[114]

And then I came across the research of Jonathan D. Sarna, a distinguished historian and Professor of American Jewish History at Brandeis University. In 1981, Dr. Sarna published his landmark book, *Jacksonian Jew: The Two Worlds of Mordecai Noah.*[115] In this globally acclaimed work that greatly expanded and enhanced my understanding of the character and accomplishments of Mordecai Noah, Sarna portrays him as a charismatic man of action deeply immersed in both American and Jewish worlds. This author had written an earlier scholarly piece about Noah as well: *"The Roots of Ararat: An Early Letter from Mordecai M. Noah to Peter B. Porter."* In fact, a bibliographic essay at the end of Sarna's book reveals a long list of many other scholarly and journalistic works written over time, many of them by Mordecai Noah.

Who was Mordecai Noah?

So who was this Mordecai Noah? And where exactly was that preliminary Zion? First of all, he was an American, born in 1765 in Philadelphia, and the son of Spanish-Portuguese *Marrano* (secret Jews) immigrants to Georgia in the New World.

Mordecai Manuel Noah had strong political and family connections in the U.S. (Among other things, he married President Andrew Jackson's daughter, Rebecca, only 17 at the time.) As the editor of an important newspaper, a journalist, playwright, dramatic speaker, and possessor of a charismatic personality, Noah rose—a

Jew in the latter part of the 18th century—to be appointed American Consul to Turkey, eventually settling in Tunis.

Many very wealthy Jews, some with surnames still recognizable today, and adept at large-scale commerce and interconnectivity, lived in North Africa at that time. They had considerable economic influence in this Muslim environment. However, there were large numbers of very poor Jews as well on the Barbary Coast, where piracy at sea was a constant threat.

While attempting to redeem white, enslaved American hostages (with Noah's usual *panache* but unexpected expense) from Barbary Coast pirates, Noah saw many cruelties that disturbed him. According to Klinger, he was deeply saddened by the deplorable and humiliating conditions in which the Jews of that area lived. After all, he had been born and brought up as a free American.

Partly because of his vigorous efforts to alleviate the conditions of the impoverished Jews in Turkey, he was soon recalled by the American government. However, the reason given for his recall—his Jewish faith—was false. Ironically, one of the reasons Mordecai Noah had been given the consular post in the first place was because he was Jewish. At the time, it was believed in diplomatic circles that Jews could be useful as consuls in Muslim countries because, as neither Christians nor Muslims, they were likely to be neutral in delicate circumstances. The American government, urgently needing to "cover up" the unexpectedly high expenses involved in ransoming the pirated ship's American captives, decided on the religious faith story to mask monies spent. It was duplicitous and personally hurtful to Noah.

Sarna, on the other hand, views Mordecai Noah's story as part of a larger picture of the making of the American Jew as a vibrant, inter-connected composite drawn from so many different forces, backgrounds, and views. In depicting this more expansive canvas in *Jacksonian Jew: The Two Worlds of Mordecai Noah*, only one chapter deals with this first consular experience. In Sarna's picture of Noah, we find a commanding figure (with some emotive foibles, it is true) who modeled personal and practical involvement and continued leadership in both the American and Jewish way of life.

Klinger's smaller study focuses more intensely on the effect of Noah's consular recall from Turkey (one weighted with antisemitic undertones). It inflamed Noah's desire to find a home for the Jewish people, Klinger claims. And, although Noah didn't succeed in his historic quest to establish a temporary refuge for the Jews on Grand Island, he lit the flame of Zionist aspirations that took hold a century later as antisemitic sentiments grew in Europe.

While for more than 2,000 years, Jewish prayers have focused attention on facing east towards Jerusalem, Mordecai Noah was likely the very first Zionist in America. He pre-dated Theodore

Herzl—usually credited with being the Father of Zionism—by a century. Mordecai Noah was not afraid to follow his dreams, not even a dream that seemed impossible at the time, but was based on an ancient promise—the promise of *Va'era* when God appears and says to the ancient Hebrews:

> "I am the LORD, I will free you from the labors of the Egyptians and deliver you from their bondage…. And I will take you to be My people, and I will be your God…. I will bring you into the land which I swore to give to Abraham, Isaac, and Jacob, and I will give it to you for a possession, I the Lord." (*Exodus 6: 6-8*).[116]

And, believing in the promise, Mordecai Manuel Noah opened the letter of his dream.

A Preliminary Refuge

Mordecai Noah believed sincerely that the Jews needed to leave the lands of their persecution, the lands where they lived in ghettos, and worse, with continual terror and death a ruler's whim away. They needed to pursue the goal—the never-forgotten dream—of living once again in their spiritual home, *Eretz Israel*, as Jews. Yet because, at that time, there were no political barriers to that dream, Mordecai Noah envisioned a *preliminary* Promised

Land, a temporary refuge until the time was right to settle in Israel. And that first place of refuge was to be an island with a small Indigenous population off the East Coast—near Buffalo, N.Y.—of the United States.

James Madison Granted Charter

It took Mordecai Noah until 1820. He was fifty-five. By then, this very able, extremely theatrical, master politician had mustered enough support to persuade the then Governor of New York State, James Madison, to grant him a charter to purchase large tracts of Grand Island (a former Canadian possession which was then ceded to New York State).

This island was located in the Niagara River near Buffalo.[117] The stated idea, with the blessing of the State of New York, was to create a temporary homeland for the persecuted Jews of the world under American protection. It was to be called Ararat (symbolizing Noah's Ark, which some people still believe to be stranded atop Mount Ararat)—and given Noah's last name and his considerable ego, he promoted the comparison. He was saving the Jews from persecution.

Economic Prospects: The Erie Canal

It wasn't all philanthropy. Since the Erie Canal was about to be opened, the location and development of Grand Island offered great economic prospects, both for the Jews who would settle there and develop it, and for the State of New York.

In this enterprise, Mordecai Noah had both the enthusiastic financial backing of devout Christians and the supportive participation of Grand Island's Seneca Indigenous population, a peaceful tribe. Mordecai Noah sincerely believed that the American Indigenous people were lost tribes of Israel, and the native population liked that idea. Grand Island was also intended to be a refuge for them against discrimination, and he planned to bring them prosperity.

But No Jews...

At the time, the Indigenous people were all for it. In fact, the only people who did not support this enterprise were the rabbis of the Jewish communities of the world, who refused completely to send any representatives to the dedication ceremony.

The Indigenous people were there at the ceremony, which took place on the mainland, dressed in full ceremonial attire. All the politicians were there, prepared to endorse the endeavor, as well as the enthusiastic Christians who had lent the money to buy the land. Mordecai Noah was there, prepared to preside over Grand Island as a judge, just like in biblical days, to get things started.

With his theatrical panache, he was dressed in ceremonial robes (rented from a costumer). The boats were all there ready to transport the invited guests to the island, despite the unexpectedly stormy weather. The only people who weren't there were the Jews, whose rabbis had been invited from all over Europe.

The island was too small to accommodate all the Jews of the world, the rabbis countered. And who wanted to live in an undeveloped wilderness? And, most important, the Messiah hadn't come yet. So despite the fact that Grand Island offered a beautiful refuge with a temperate climate, it wasn't *Eretz Israel*. And despite the fact that Mordecai Noah explained that the refuge was planned to be temporary in nature— until one day they could move safely to the Holy Land—nevertheless, for the rabbis, it was Israel or bust. They had no idea that a Holocaust would decimate the European Jewish communities in the twentieth century. If it wasn't Israel, the rabbis declared, not a single Jew except for Mordecai Noah was coming to the dedication. Nevertheless, the dedication ceremony did take place, and the cornerstone still rests today in Grand Island's museum.

Mordecai Noah was born just after the close of the first American Revolution. He died in 1851, a few years before the Civil War— the War Between the States— began. When he died, he was still a dedicated Zionist. But he had come to the realization in the thirty years after the Grand Island venture failed in its intent, that, for the Jews of the world, Zion had to be in Israel.

Despite his exhausting efforts, Mordecai Noah could not achieve his goal of finding a place for the Jews. But he created a defined goal for the Jewish people: the only place they wanted to create a land for the Jews, the only place they wanted to find refuge, was in *Eretz Israel*, the land biblically promised to them by God. No other land would do. Zionism—and the eventual establishment of Israel—was on its way.

> (4) "And the LORD said to him, 'This is the land of which I swore to Abraham, Isaac, and Jacob, I will assign it to your offspring. I have let you see it with your own eyes, but you shall not cross there.' (5) So Moses, the servant of the LORD died there, in the land of Moab, at the command of the Lord." (Deut. 34: 4-5)[118]

The Dream of the Generations

The story of Mordecai Noah reminds us that we stand on the shoulders of our heroes through time to make the world a better place. The goals he tried so valiantly to attain—in accordance with the visual picture of the Promised Land proclaimed by God— would be achieved by the generations to follow.

I was 12 years old in May, 1948, as our family gathered around the radio (there was no television yet in Canada) to listen to

David Ben Gurion courageously proclaiming Israel's Declaration of Independence from afar (the next day five Arab armies would attack Israel) at a time long before the Internet made instantaneous communication from far-off lands commonplace. It was an electric moment that I have never forgotten, an emotional connection with the Holy Land that cannot be replicated by reading about history.

The Dream Realized

Of course, it took many others who dreamed the dream of generations after Mordecai Noah to make it happen. It took dedicated people like Dr. Theodor Herzl who spent his life (which sadly ended with a heart attack at the age of 44) helping the dream of generations come to fruition. During the summer of 2022, I watched the Simon Wiesenthal Center's excellent documentary film about Herzl, "It's No Dream," and, although I already knew the details of his life's endeavor and the progression of his dream, I still found myself very moved.

Initially, who would have thought that a secular Jew—a playwright and journalist who lived in Vienna, who came to Paris to report on the infamous Captain Alfred Dreyfus trial—would become so incensed by the fabricated accusations of military espionage leveled against Dreyfus because he was Jewish? Dreyfus' humiliation and court martial took place at a time of growing antisemitism spreading not only in Paris but all over Europe. Herzl realized that it was useless for Jewish people to try so hard to "fit in" to European civilization, to try so hard to be other than they were. The script was already written, had been written for centuries; Jews would always be political and religious scapegoats in difficult times. It would always be *"Juden Raus"* in Berlin and elsewhere: Kick them out and seize their property and other assets.

There was no other choice, Herzl believed. It was time for the Jewish people to live in their own land, hopefully at peace. So he wrote his ideas down, first in a working paper and then as a book called *Der Judenstat*,[119] providing a modern (at that time) solution to the Jewish persecution problem. When 500 copies of the book were published, Herzl was ecstatic, and the idea of a Jewish state as a reality took hold among the Jewish people.

The big problem, as Mordecai Noah discovered earlier, was "Where?" Where should the Jewish people go to make the dream into reality? As the SWC's documentary film sets out so beautifully, the obvious answer, for both historical and religious reasons, was to return to Israel. Sadly, Herzl was to encounter both disinterest or outright opposition from many directions—politicians, the elite rich among the Jews, Orthodox rabbis waiting for the Messiah, and Reform rabbis who thought the better path was to achieve outright integration. The Turks took his money gladly, but to no avail. With tremendous effort, he managed to get an audience with Kaiser Wilhelm of Austria, who insisted on meeting in Jerusalem, but when the Kaiser viewed the squalor and poverty of that city and its inhabitants at that time, he changed his mind about offering any support. Jerusalem then was not the beautiful city it is today as part of the State of Israel.

Still, Herzl did not give up. Eventually, he was to find his support, not from the very rich, but from the everyday people, from the poor Jews and the *Hasids* of Eastern Europe. Finally, in 1897, Herzl realized that the time was right to organize the First World Zionist Congress in Basel, a tremendous effort and, as it turned out, a great success. There would be many more Zionist Congresses to follow, as well as intricate international negotiations before the State of Israel could be proclaimed. At one point, Mordecai Noah reluctantly accepted the offer of Uganda as a temporary stop gap, but it was not to be. The dream was in Israel. "If I forget thee, O Jerusalem, let my right hand wither." (Psalm 137: 5-6)[120]

There would be many other courageous, dedicated leaders, of course, who would follow in Theodor Herzl's footsteps. Yet, as the documentary film depicts, both David Ben Gurion and Shimon Perez proclaimed, upon taking office in the new Jewish state, Israel, that it was Theodor Herzl who should really be recognized as the first Prime Minister of Israel.

And, I would add, the "ordinary" people—like the anonymous older women I witnessed at a meeting of Pioneer Women in Canada, who did not have money to donate when the fledgling state was attacked by Arab armies in 1945—they should be celebrated too. With tears in both their eyes and mine, I watched them take off their gold wedding rings and place them in the collection box for Israel. I was only nine years old, but I understood what they were really giving—their whole hearts.

Mordecai Noah was unable to complete his dream, but he initiated a process that would be resumed not only by Herzl but by countless others, and a century and a half later, the dream would come to be.

An oft-repeated Jewish maxim from the *Pirkei Avot: Ethics of Our Fathers* explains that *"You are not obligated to complete the work, but neither are you free to desist from it."*[121] Eventually, generation after generation of Jewish people continuously working together did complete the task. Half a century after Herzl died, they re-established ancient Israel and rebuilt it into a modern state. In Israel. Now the task is for Jews living today, despite all the difficulties, to support the work of generations.

My guess is that many young Jewish people in America and elsewhere have never had the opportunity to read Israel's Declaration of Independence. The full text is included in Appendix 2 of this book. I have transcribed the words as they appear on the plaque given to my father in appreciation of his own efforts to help Israel reach this day—"the dream of the generations"—on May 14, 1948.

YERUSHALAYIM: CITY OF PEACE[122]

God, You have shown me

Your wineglass in a

Blessed city that wishes

The world what it might be.

O Jerusalem, for me

You plant new vineyards

In the cloudless sky.

   —Corinne Copnick

Redemption and the State of Israel

In his historical article, "Hope Jewish and Hope Secular," Eugene B. Borowitz laments the declining influence of the Talmud as secular stances increased after the Enlightenment.[123] Concepts of hope changed after the Enlightenment, he stresses. From the end of the 18th century, coinciding with the establishment of the secular state and with rights for Jews as citizens, Judaism underwent a steady process of secularization. Social and intellectual pressures increased, religious faith took a further beating, and the secular hope for the future redefined itself as "the enhancement of man's capabilities."[124] This secular stance brought with it questions about hope as well. Firstly, is hope possible without faith in God? Secondly, are the expectations of secular hope different from religious hope?

It is often said that Judaism is an action religion. The concept of "to listen and to do" is as old as the giving of the Torah on Mount Sinai. And the covenant is still our framework.... Prayer, yes (the rabbinic substitute for sacrifices after the Temples were destroyed), but, in the opinion of many today, passive waiting, no! It died in the face of persecution, torture, and murder with the victims of the ghettos and the concentration camps of the Holocaust.[125]

As a result of the increased secularization of religion in both Israel and the Diaspora, Reform Judaism incorporates a huge emphasis on Social Action as a *raison d'etre*. Today, for Jewish

Rabbi Corinne Copnick

people everywhere—ranging from secular to orthodox—no matter what the religious model, vision, or time frame, the do-able plan involves courage, dedication, and commitment. Referred to as *tikkun olam* (repairing the world), it has remained relevant to all streams of Judaism. It's an action intention that involves the sense of ethical and spiritual purpose that makes life worth living. It promotes faith in humanity, and "faith," as David R. Blumenthal asserts, "includes faithfulness."[126]

TRANSPLANTED[127]

I found a tree that feels like me,

all flame and autumn fire,

dark branches reaching fine-honed

fingers to hold the wistful sky.

I touched a tree whose roots go deep,

proudly placed by sturdy stones,

moistly loved by velvet earth,

tall grown to sanctify this day.

I touched a tree whose time has come,

whose color gladly bares herself

to winter's gutsy grasp and

guards her blazing power,

transplanted in the night.

—*Corinne Copnick*

CHAPTER 10

DIVERSITY, EQUITY, AND INCLUSION

IN THE LANGUAGE OF HOPE

INCLUSION: YARZHEIT, 2017

OUR HOPE

A FABLE FOR OUR TIME

*I*n recent years, there has been a tremendous political and societal emphasis, especially among the current generation, on diversity, equity, and inclusion. Political correctness in new ways of speaking and new pronouns for gender identity have become the norm. Every generation brings in new ways of thinking, speaking, or being. It must make its own impact on the world. Sometimes the new way of societal behavior and thought goes too far, though, with "cancel culture," for instance. Either you are "woke" or you are not, and if you are not, there is no place for you. it has become commonplace to say that political—and ethnic and color—divisions have reached an aggressive level this country has not seen since the Civil War. In an unfortunate throwback to the past, even the civil rights of half of humanity—women—are being assaulted. Old tyrannies revived are cloaked in new language. These divisions cannot stand.

Jews have long understood that, from the time of the naming of the animals in the Garden of Eden, the Jewish tradition has celebrated diversity. Strangers—*gerim* in Hebrew—are to be treated well. There is even a special prayer, a blessing Jews are commanded to say when they see a person who looks "different" or who has a disability. In Hebrew the prayer sounds like this: *"Baruch Atah Adonai Eloheinu Melech Ha-Olam Meshaneh Habriot."* The prayer is one of gratitude for seeing people or creatures who are very special or unique in their appearances. It thanks God for creating difference.

Sometimes these "different" people are just very fat, obese in fact, like my late sister who had Type I uncontrollable diabetes from childhood, "brittle" diabetes, the doctor called it when it was finally diagnosed when she became an adult. Eventually the disease attacked every organ in her body until she succumbed to the illness and died. She never realized that she had a beautiful face and a beautiful soul.

INCLUSION: YARTZHEIT, 2017[128]

a beautiful body is a lovely thing

an admirable value my sister didn't

have a beautiful body she felt

left out I know what it did

to my sister inside

b'ahavah

—*Corinne Copnick*

Rabbi Corinne Copnick

There are similar prayers for experiencing other wonders of nature: lightning, hearing thunder, seeing a colorful rainbow—or experiencing the ocean or large body of water for the first time, or a tree blossom in the spring. In other words, we should experience wonder at the awesome creativity of nature. Why don't we thank God for people of different colors?

In fact, one of the many reasons that I was interested in participating for several years, as both a *dayan* (judge in Hebrew) and Governor of the Sandra Caplan Community *Bet Din*[129] (rabbinic court of law) in respect to conversion is because of the respect this multi-denominational (Reform, Conservative, Reconstructionist, Trans-denominational) group of Los Angeles area rabbis gives to this concept of diversity and inclusion and considers it in their decision-making about conversion. In particular, under the leadership of Chaplain Muriel Dance, Ph.D., and our SCCBD Board, a great effort has been made to welcome and integrate new Jews of Color not only into the Jewish community at large, but into a Jewish community of their own choosing and comfort. The same welcome has been extended to members of the LGBTQ+ community.

When they have an opportunity to visit Israel, these new Jews will find plenty of diversity there as well. Today Israel is home, not only to the descendants of early pioneers who "made the desert bloom" again, nor to aged European Jews who somehow survived dire persecution during World War II and

134

their *Sabra* children, grandchildren and great grandchildren, but also—according to the long-established American Jewish Committee, to "Jews from all over the globe, including Jews fleeing persecution from the Soviet Union, the Arab world, Turkey, Iran, and Ethiopia, amongst others. Israel is one of the most diverse countries in the world with over half of its population being from Africa, India, and other areas of the Middle East. The vast majority of Jews around the world identify as Zionists, meaning they support the existence of Israel as a Jewish state in the historic Land of Israel."[130]

The Jews of the world are non-binary in relation to skin color—not divided into whites or blacks. Or shades of brown, for that matter. Or any other color. Like Joseph in the Bible, Jews are blessed with a coat of many colors. And they are blessed in belonging to an ancient people with a deep yearning expressed in their prayers for this holy land, Israel. At every age, no matter where they live in reality, spiritually Jews remain *B'nai Israel*, the children of Israel.[131]

* * * *

I want so much to convey to Generation Z, to my grandchildren, how much the land of Israel has meant, continues to mean, to Jews who live everywhere. It is our historic and spiritual homeland. To Jews who live in Israel, it is their actual, physical home, the one they must defend on a daily basis. To all of us, religious or secular, no matter where we dwell, Israel remains our eternal hope, our perpetual reminder of the values our ancestors undertook to uphold in the biblical Covenant on Sinai. Israel is not simply a physical place, a small dot in the geography of the world. It is a reminder that the land is not yours nor mine nor any of the civilizations that have tried to possess it over thousands of years. The land belongs to God the Creator, and it represents the hope of what the world might be, a project undertaken by the Jewish people thousands of years ago and still to be completely fulfilled. That's why Israel's national anthem is called *Hatikvah*, "The Hope."[132] Here are the words, much loved by many Jews, excoriated by some, translated into English:

THE HOPE

Here is the English translation: [133]

"As long as in the heart within,

The Jewish soul yearns,

And toward the eastern edges, onward,

An eye gazes toward Zion.

"Our hope is not yet lost,

The hope that is two-thousand years old,

To be a free nation in our land,

The Land of Zion, Jerusalem."

And here is the English-language transliteration of the Hebrew:[134]

Kol od balevav penimah,

Nefesh yehudi homiyah,

Ukefa-atei mizrach, kadimah,

Ayin letziyon tsofiyah.

Od lo avdah tikvateinu,

Hatikva bat shnot alpayim,

Lihyot am chofshi be-artzeinu,

Eretz tzion, virushalayim

In an era when appreciation of diversity is a topic of public contemplation, I find it so interesting that most people I encounter love animals of different breeds or colors. Strange, isn't it, that we can enjoy the natural, diverse beauty of animals—oh, the stripes of the tiger—yet find our differences a sticking point when it comes to human beings? Why should animals have all the fun? After all, we humans are all created beings. I would like to think that in this 21st century, we are finally making strides in our acceptance of people who don't look like "us," or communicate like us. Or think like us.

It is in this spirit that I offer the following story, "A Fable For Our Time," which really happened to me when I was a young girl. It is what the movies would call "a heart-warming tale," and I have read it to appreciative audiences ever since.

A Fable for our Time

"How do you know that your blood is redder than his, perhaps his blood is redder than yours?" (Rava in *Sanhedrin 74a, Talmud.*)

I didn't know yet when I was eleven years old that the Talmud teaches that every life has value. I learned it by example from an animal, from my pet cat, Buttons. She was a beautiful Persian cat with piercing green eyes and fur so glossy and black it seemed to have purple highlights. Naturally she attracted the attention of some of the neighborhood Toms, and soon we noticed that Buttons seemed heavier around her middle.

Then one evening as I was taking a bath, I heard sounds behind the tile bathroom walls, faint sounds. Mice? No, they seemed to be mewing sounds...behind the wall. Wrapping my towel around me, I rushed to the cupboard just outside our bathroom. Sure enough, the cover to the opening of the wide pipe that ran behind the bathroom wall had been chewed off. I put my ear to the pipe and listened. Yes, those sounds were alive, and, oh, the heated air was warm in there.

With eleven-year-old valor, I reached my hand in as far as I could and touched...wet fur. That is how I lifted out, first one, then two little kittens. But I could still hear a faint mewing. Stretching my arm to the limit, I reached in once more and lifted out a third kitten. Jubilant, I carried them all downstairs to our warm kitchen and settled them comfortably in a basket lined with soft towels. My little sister instantly named them Spic, Span, and Rainbow. Spic was white, Span was black, and Rainbow was multi-colored.

I thought Buttons would be so pleased to see her kittens safe and sound in the basket. But she was not pleased. No, she was frantic as she touched each of them on the nose and paused. And then again, she counted noses. Then she rushed up the stairs to the bathroom closet and squeezed into the warm pipe. She soon emerged with one kitten (Blondie, we called her because she was a strawberry-blonde), and then with another (Tawny, the color of *café au lait*). She carried them down one by one to the kitchen basket, and when all five of them were settled, she counted their noses with her own nose. ONE-TWO-THREE-FOUR-FIVE. And then again to make sure. That's how she took her own census. I didn't know that cats could count, but they do if it concerns their own children. Finally, she settled contentedly into the basket with her furry kittens – like the biblical Joseph's coat, a magnificent blend of many colors.

That's how I learned from one of God's small creatures—a black cat with diverse children, each of whom she loved—that every life counts. As the Torah teaches, and poets have always known, each star, each grain of sand, each human life matters. Everywhere.

And for the precious gift of our lives, we owe it to God and to ourselves to make every minute, every hour count. To use it well for ourselves in the time that we have—something we especially appreciate as we grow older—and to use it well for other lives that have been created, for humanity and for all of God's creatures.

Internalizing that concept, teaching it to our children, and putting it into action, that's what gives us hope. Even when circumstances take a downturn, we have faith that one day—if we all pull together—they'll get better. That's the miracle.

CHAPTER 11

HOPE AS A MIRACLE

YOU ARE MINE

FRUTAS?

CHAYA

Do Jews Really Believe in Miracles?

*"D*o Jews believe in miracles?" This question, in fact, was asked in an excellent and simply written article that can be found online in *My Jewish Learning's Virtual Library*.[135] It seems that, as a people, indeed we do. "From the Bible to the Talmud to the Hasidic masters, miracles are found everywhere in Jewish tradition—but there is no single way to understand them."

The Hebrew word for miracle, *nes*, as *My Jewish Learning* explains, is usually translated as a "sign," signaling an uncommon and sometimes dramatic change directly brought about by God in the course of our worldly events throughout the generations. Sometimes the biblical God worked through human agents. In the classical rabbinic period, a body of folklore grew up about miracles, but the medieval period saw a more rationalistic approach take over, with Maimonides insisting that seemingly miraculous things are really part of the natural, preordained order of the universe.

With the rise of Hassidic *rebbes* led by the Bal Shem Tov in the Early Modern period, the concept of "personal miracle workers" grew. However, in the "Modern" period in which we live today, there are many different approaches to miracles. Traditionally, Judaism welcomes multiple views. And the hope for a miracle extends to all people, any place, anywhere. And may heaven always help you!

You are mine![136]

In the last year of the 1970s, my husband and I had traveled to Mexico on holiday. In particular, we visited *Cancun*, which had recently been clawed from the jungle in order to develop that beautiful, ocean-side site into an eventual tourist mecca. What I especially wanted to visit, however, was *Chitzen Itza*, the religious site of a once flourishing Mayan civilization. Although we had to travel on dirt roads through the jungle at the time, it was possible to get there from *Cancun*.

We had been told in advance that the experience carried with it mystical connotations (precisely why I wanted to visit). As we were taken by our Mayan guide to the massive ruins inlaid with turquoise and carvings, that really must be visited rather than described, unsettling questions came to mind. How could a once primitive culture construct those huge stones in the jungle? Was the terrain different then? Did people from another planet build and become an integral part of this past? How to explain the combination of astrological science with barbaric cruelty? How to account for the sophisticated mathematical calculations of natives capable of sacrificing their own people, human beings, to their gods that came first?

What did God mean in that place, amid that architectural wonder?

I was astonished when the Mayan guide, looking intently at the small Star of David I always wear around my neck, leaned forward and spoke to me in Hebrew (a language I only started learning at the age of 72).

His dark eyes flashed in an encounter I have thought about for years. His white teeth shone in what appeared to be a Mayan-hued face. "You are my people," he said. "We are the same. Books have been written about us. We came here as a lost tribe."

Was he descended from the *Marranos*, Jews who were forced to keep their faith secret to escape persecution during the Spanish Inquisition—seemingly converted Jews who fled to Mexico?

"Where did you learn Hebrew?" I gasped.

"My family has always known it," he replied almost ecstatically. "I am Mayan, and you are mine," he said.

He was my tour guide, but he would not accept money from me. I was his.

That encounter was a long time ago. A decade or so later, in 1992, a divorced middle-aged lady now, I had traveled once again to Mexico, this time alone. Now I was returning home from a stay at the famed artist's colony in *San Miguel Allende* and seated on a bus beside a matronly Mexican lady. "I'm descended from the Toltecs, not the Mayans," she told me.

As I looked around the bus, I realized for the first time that most of the passengers appeared to be Indigenous to Mexico.

Suddenly I felt a surge of affection for my seat mate. "Are you also mine?" I wondered. "Is that why I feel so close to you? Is that why, coming from such different cultures, with such poor grasp of each other's languages, we converse so easily on the bus?"

"Or are you mine because you are a kind human being, because your time-worn face is creased with laugh lines, because for you God is first?"

I wanted so much to communicate my feelings, but I didn't have the words in Spanish.

* * * *

The need to know the language had possessed me before I ever got on the first-class bus (at that time, second-class buses had no bathrooms, and the trip back to the Mexico City airport was five hours). During my stay at *San Miguel de Allende*, I attended poetry readings and lectures on literature and art in English, but I had also signed up for daily language classes at the *Instituto Allende*.

"In Mexico there is much concentration on religion," my language teacher at the *Instituto* explained in Spanish. "At Christmas the importance is placed on the nativity, not on gift-giving, because many families have no money."

"Despite this, Mexican families look after their own," my teacher went on. "There are no nursing homes. It is up to the family to look after the old parents."

"Then why are there beggars at the church?" I asked, using gestures where I lacked the words. It was beyond pitiful to see those withered old creatures, bent and barely able to walk, mostly women, hanging around the churches decorated with godly images in bright colors, and with people in the pews at almost any time of day.

I had seen destitute people asking for money before: the gypsies in Spain who paint their children's faces with chalk to elicit sympathy for their plight; the children in the Dominican Republic who can't go to school because they have no shoes. In Israel once, a woman thrust her hand into the passenger window of my taxi in her desperation for money. I have seen the misery of the homeless who sleep in tents or on the streets, even in the USA. But I have never seen beggars as broken as these old women pleading for *pesos*. No one should have to live like that. Not in Mexico, not anywhere.

When I left *San Miguel*, I left most of my wardrobe behind for these poor people, these *"pobres,"* dresses, slacks, and even, forgetting the price of Adidas at home, my running shoes. I left them at the church.

Yet in the language classroom, my teacher shrugged at my passion. "Mexicans think these people did not give love to their children," she rationalized. "If they had given love to their children, the children would look after them. They would live with their children. Or even if the children move away and this is not possible,

Mexican children will pay someone to look after their parents in their parents' home, so the neighbors are not disturbed. Mexicans do not like to put their parents in nursing homes. When someone is in a nursing home, we think their children have thrown them away. Why do their children not want them?"

My seat companion on the bus was full of love. Surely, her children would want to take care of her in her old age. I knew they would help her.

Frutas[137]

Time had passed. It was the 1990's, and, after more than a quarter of a century, I was no longer married. I knew my own grown children would always help me, just as, with love, I had helped my own parents. But, locked in the bathroom of the first-class bus on the way to Mexico City, they were too far away. I was a writer, traveling sadly back from *San Miguel's* famed art colony alone because my father in Canada was dying. Long past his ability to recognize his loved ones, there was no further help we could give to my father. I knew I would be going back to his funeral. And now I was trapped in the bathroom of the bus.

"*Ayudame*," I cried out to strangers from another culture. "Please help me open the door! It's stuck!"

Would I understand enough Spanish to grasp the replies? "*Vuelve...*" I heard. "*Vuelve...*" I was already trying over and over to turn the lock. It wouldn't move. *"No vuelve,"* I almost sobbed. The voices screamed louder, but the Spanish I might have understood was lost in the even louder sounds of the road.

My ear pressed to the door, I tried in vain to make out what the cacophony of voices was now trying to tell me.

Suddenly, the bus ground to a halt. Silence. Apparently, the bus driver had had enough. He strode down the aisle of the bus and knocked on the door. *"Vuelve AL DERECHO,"* he directed in a voice that could now be heard.

"I've been turning and turning *to the LEFT*," I cried. "I can't move the lock."

"Vuelve MAS!" the small group now at the door shouted. "Turn it *MORE*!"

With this amassed confidence and the voice of authority, the driver, at the door, I summoned all my strength and, cutting my finger in the process, *TURNED* the lock to the left. As it opened, I mentally calculated the last time I had been given a tetanus shot.

As I exited sheepishly, a seated row of faces-turned-over-their-shoulders gazed at me, big grins on their faces. The Indigenous ladies were unabashedly giggling at me. I smiled back.

"Gracias" I said, holding on to my dignity, as the bus driver shook his head in disbelief at this *gringa*, and the entire bus collapsed in laughter.

Rabbi Corinne Copnick

I reached down in my travel bag and pulled out a bag of dried apricots. I had bought them at the marketplace in *San Miguel* where Indigenous families sit on blankets removing the spines from cacti with large, sharp knives before they are cut up with green beans to be sold as vegetables. I had soaked the apricots very carefully in purified water for three days before securing them in a plastic bag.

"*Frutas,*" I asked, passing the bag of apricots to my friends, the Indigenous ladies. They had shouted "*Vuelve AL DERECHO*" loudest at the bathroom door. They accepted smilingly and pronounced the apricots very good indeed. I was theirs. They were mine. It was a little miracle.

Chaya the Shoichet (Chicken-Killer)[138]

I never meant to choose a dog like Chaya. When I first saw her early in the morning, Chaya was still grieving the loss of her previous owner, but she was a long-haired vision of Arctic beauty. A Samoyed husky. I stroked her white, silky hair and talked to her gently. I told her in soft tones how much I needed someone to love. The day went by without even the faintest acknowledgement of my repeated overtures. Several times I walked away, but each time returned.

It was an event outside myself that propelled me to seek a dog. I not only needed a companion, I needed a protector; for an ugly episode had taken place in my very own driveway. The sanctity of my comfortable white stucco and terracotta home was violated by a crude, little note, hand-lettered carefully on yellow, lined, foolscap paper: "This is for the animals who died to make your mink coat."

The four tires of my car had been irreparably slashed. With malice aforethought. Right in my driveway. The nasty note had been placed under the rear wheel of my car. "Maybe you should get a dog," the young, blue-eyed policeman had said.

So when I went down to the Humane Society, it was with determination. "Doggie," I persuaded, as I returned to the cage for the sixth time. "It's the middle of the afternoon. Open your eyes. I am here."

This time she responded to my voice, looked at me with her beguiling, velvety-black eyes. Delicately, she licked the tips of my fingers, extended towards her through the cage wires.

That did it! She was everything that was wrong for me, but the moment she kissed my hand, we were a match. It was love at first sight.

I had wanted a sizeable dog that looked fierce, a dog who would ward off would-be assailants with a loud bark, not a pile of black and white fluff. But when I saw Chaya, in her silky-haired mourning attire in the shelter's cage, it was instant identification. Her name, "Chaya," was tacked to the front of the cage. She had lost her family. When Chaya was eight years old, her mistress had a baby, and Chaya grew jealous of the baby. It was a choice between the dog or the baby.

So there she lay, mortified, the most beautiful dog in the world, locked in a cage at the Humane Society. "Eight years old," I pondered. A dog's age is calculated at about seven dog years for every year of human life. It was doubtful she would find another home.

"She's a wonderful dog," the attendant said. "Well trained. She just got jealous. She's even been trained not to bark.

When the attendant told me she had a bit of arthritis in her back legs, I knew that despite the fact she didn't meet most of my requirements, she was made for me. So what if she looked like a marshmallow, not a fierce protector! So what if she didn't bark? It was *bechert*! Destiny!

"We'll watch our diets and exercise together," I mused. "Did you come from a kosher home?" I inquired directly into Chaya's ear. Her eyes remained closed, but Chaya's graceful upswept Samoyed tail showed the hint of a wag.

"Chaya," I sweet-talked the dog, "my Jewish name is just like yours. Chaya. Animal. We have the same name." Did I imagine that the dog's ears perked up for the first time. "*Chayele*," I coaxed, using the Yiddish diminutive. "Little Animal, I love you."

It was at that moment Chaya opened her eyes and kissed my hand. She knew she was loved. She knew she was mine. She had found a good Jewish home. And as I patted her head and pressed my face against her soft fur, I knew that she was my little miracle.

I took Chaya everywhere. To the post office, the drug store, the shoe store, and to my aunt's for dinner. She had tidbits under the table and shared my morning toast with me. At the corner bakery, they gave her *pareve* cookies while she waited outside. Everywhere people petted her. I even took her with me to the hairdresser. They brushed her silky hair, too. Chaya loved going to the hairdresser.

So when a friend invited me to attend an exhibit at a native art gallery, it seemed only natural to take Chaya, too. The art gallery was located at the edge of a First Nations Reserve in the Ontario countryside in Canada. The artwork shown there was the creation of Indigenous artists. One of the artists, a petite, round-faced quilt-maker of some international renown, invited the charming friend and myself to dinner.

They had known one another for a long time. Little Animal was welcome, too. In the rugged expanse of rural wilderness that framed the reserve, Little Animal was soon to become Wild Animal. *Vilde Chaya*, as it is called in Yiddish.

The country lake was the first thing to evoke Chaya's primitive inner voice. She was part husky, after all. She dove into the water in the late day, just as the sun was beginning to dip itself into the lake. Little Animal swam as if the lake and sun and trees belonged to her. She shook her fur when she emerged and frisked happily with the large dog belonging to our Indigenous hosts.

"City dog?" one of our hosts asked, raising a skeptical, bushy eyebrow. He was the quilt-maker's husband and wore a leather, fringed jacket. "I don't think so. Country dog," he pronounced. My friend, an environmental consultant by profession, smiled at me. He was at home in these surroundings. His white mustache quivered with pleasure.

I smiled back. "Like your people and mine," I answered our host, "Chaya has a long history.

Then we happily sat down with ten or more First Nations people at long, rough wood tables for a barbecue. The pickerel cooked over an open fire, and the roasted potatoes smelled delicious. Green beans from the garden adorned the salad. But in this ecological heaven, we ate on paper plates with plastic utensils, and drank from paper cups.

"*L'chaim*," I offered a toast over the bush tea, brewed strong over the fire. In response, they taught me some words in Ojibway, almost a lost language.

As home-baked apple and blueberry pies were brought to the table, one of the native men laughed happily. "Whenever we had dessert, my Mama always said, "Just turn over the plates, kids, and eat on the other side." Everyone giggled and turned their paper plates upside down to receive the slices of pie.

"Do you want a little piece of pie, Chaya?" I reached under the table to give my slice to the dog. Chaya had taken her place under the table as the meal began, her nose close to my feet, so I could slip her little tidbits from time to time. This time there was no receiving, moist dog tongue. Chaya wasn't there. During all the merriment, she had slipped away.

Hurriedly, I began to look for her. Here, in this country setting, amongst aboriginal people with a past so closely connected to the land, had my eight-year-old, Jewish husky responded to some primeval urge and returned to the wilderness?

Rabbi Corinne Copnick

"Chaya," I cupped my fingers to my mouth to enlarge the sound. "*Chayele,*" I called. "Where are you? This is your Jewish mother asking. Come back."

I remembered how my grandmother used to tie a horsehair ring around her finger to keep away the evil eye. In these strange surroundings, had an evil spirit overtaken my Chaya? Would I ever see her again? I wished that I had a horsehair ring or a five-fingered hand on a little gold chain around my neck, or an Indian dream catcher, or...at least I was wearing my *Mogen Dovid* (Jewish star).

Just then I caught a glimpse of her white tail soaring in the air amidst the tall grass. She hadn't run far away at all. There she was in a fenced enclosure behind the large, rambling house. "Oh," I sighed in relief, "she must have leaped over the fence or burrowed under it. Then the moment of relief ended as I saw what was at the front of Chaya's tail.

A chicken. Chaya had it in her mouth.

As I screamed, "No, no, not the chicken," in one fell swoop Chaya became a *shoichet* (a ritual slaughterer who koshers the meat). She had slaughtered the chicken.

Shaking the dog by her collar, I made her drop the chicken, uneaten, but it was too late. The chicken was dead.

My dinner companions heard my screams, and all ten came running. "Are you all right? Are you all right?" They gathered

156

around me protectively, and then suddenly there was silence. Everyone stared at the chicken lying on the ground.

"I'm awfully sorry," I said unhappily, "but my dog has slaughtered one of your chickens. I'll replace it."

"Oh no," my hostess gasped. Her quilter's hands flew to clasp her round cheeks. "I hope it isn't Goldie. Oh, I bet it's Goldie. I forgot that she was loose. I forgot to put her back in the hen house." Now the hands clutched her bosom as if in prayer, as she moved forward to identify the chicken.

"Goldie," her husband cried in dismay, bending down to look at the chicken, bushy brows knitted together. "Goldie is...was our pet. Most chickens only live for three or four years, but Goldie was ten years old." He looked away, his eyes almost, but not quite, misting over. "I guess it's dumb to have a chicken for a pet.

"I guess your Goldie is irreplaceable," I rejoined sadly. "Oh Chaya," I thought. "We have spoiled such a nice invitation."

"Come with me," I snapped to my dog the Assassin, and I tied her to the leg of one of the wooden banquet tables. And now Chaya, the gentle dog who never barked, found her voice. She barked and whined and whimpered.

"Be quiet," I commanded. In response, she howled non-stop like a timber wolf. "Aah-ooooh!" Or an Arctic husky reclaiming her land. Is it possible that within this mortifying tragedy, we were also witnessing a miraculous transformation? The reclamation of her true self? Finally, we prepared to take our leave.

"I hope you will invite me again," I ventured. Chaya, now sweetly on her lead ready to go home to the wilds of suburban Toronto, wagged her tail. My friend, the environmentalist, gave me a hug.

"It doesn't matter. It's just a chicken," they all assured me sadly. Everybody looked at Goldie still lying on the ground. Then my host gathered up Goldie's remains and brought them to the kitchen. He put them on the wood block beside the stove. He was a practical man. Goldie would soon be ten-year-old chicken soup.

I picked up my forgotten cup of bush tea in the paper cup and made a parting toast: *"L'chaim*, Goldie. To life! May your spirit sleep in protected bays."

CHAPTER 12

FAITH IS THE FLAME THAT KEEPS HOPE ALIVE

THE HOPE OF MRS. MANDELBAUM

MOVING ON?

*I*n Eastern Canada, where I was born and lived most of my life, November is a bleak month. After the brief autumn blaze of color, the trees have lost all their leaves, the skies are grey after the morning darkness, and snow has not yet come to whiten the landscape. People in Canada tend to get somewhat depressed in November. I used to alleviate these feelings by creating a beautiful image for myself: The trees were simply waiting, their bare branches upraised, to receive the snow that would fall in December. "Everything is waiting to be hallowed by man," Simon Noveck explains, capturing the essence of Martin Buber's theology.[139] This is how Buber felt about the relationship between God, man, and nature. And, in the final analysis, that is what hope is all about, having faith in this relationship.

Anyone who has experienced nature's astonishing "superbloom" in Spring, 2023 can surely understand. Yet long before the technology of the internet helped anyone with a computer, tablet, or smart phone to understand what it means to be "connected," the Jewish tradition understood that interaction. It understood that everything in creation, every action, is interrelated, and that in the Spring, new shoots would come. The bare branches would have leaves again.

* * * *

"Scientifically, there can be no miracles. True," writes Rabbi Maurice Lamm in his book, *The Power of Hope: The One Essential of*

Life and Love. "But science is a miracle!" he adds. "...And hope—is hope not a miracle?"[140] Rabbi Lamm's views coincide with mine.

Yet sometimes miracles need a helping hand—and considerable perseverance. "In the Talmudic concept of hope," writes Rabbi David Hartman, taking these thoughts a step further, "man bears witness to God's presence in history by persevering in the struggle for justice."[141] Continuing this theme, as noted earlier is the Reform Movement's emphasis on Social Justice, *Tikkun Olam,* repairing the world.

While it's a rabbi's job to help others with their personal distress, they also must cope with difficult moments in their own lives and that of those close to them.

How do Rabbis keep hoping?

Several books published in recent years, among them already mentioned Rabbi Maurice Lamm's *The Power of Hope* and Rabbi Naomi Levy's *Hope Will Find You: My Search for the Wisdom to Stop Waiting and Start Living*, deal in highly personal terms with the duality of hope and despair. Both authors describe different medical conditions that befell their children, and the period of utter hopelessness these difficult situations engendered. Earlier, Rabbi Harold Kushner responded to the illness and death of his young son from a degenerative disease in *Why Bad Things Happen to Good People*, which hit a popular chord and remains an enduring tool in the battle to retain one's faith in the face of adversity. Rabbi David J. Wolpe also wrote feelingly about his own continuing battle with two kinds of cancer, while trying to comfort his wife (afflicted with cancer as well) and minister to his congregation.

Yet all these authors are rabbis, as I am, whose life purpose is purportedly to teach and counsel others. So how does a rabbi (or any member of the clergy) cling to faith in a situation that fosters doubt? How does a rabbi deal with his or her own hopelessness? In his honest article, "My Last Cancer Treatment," Rabbi David Wolpe writes, "'How does one live, Rabbi?' [That] is the question my congregants ask, if not so directly. 'Tell me, Rabbi—is your job to know.'"[142] This is the answer Rabbi Wolpe provides: "Live as if you are fine, knowing that you are not...I am grateful for the time I have been given...I owe it to my family, my community, and to God not to be done before I am really done." [143]

Like Rabbi Wolpe, many members of the clergy have described a personal journey from brokenness to inner strength and faith, as each of them heartbreakingly climbed with baby steps not only to function fully in the world but also to teach and help others once again.

In her uplifting book, *Hope Will Find You*, Rabbi Naomi Levy explains that:

"Transformation requires effort from below.... and the hand from above and the hand from below have to meet in the middle."[144] And she questions: To what extent do we change ourselves, and to what degree is it helpful or necessary to have helping hands from others? These are big questions! Still, Levy's assurance by the latter part of her book that "hope will find you" will surely be a comfort to many people.[145]

At this writing, it's been a tough almost three years so far, and the pandemic challenge of this decade, the multiplicity of infectious viruses, hasn't completely ended yet at this writing. My hope is that our collective Jewish wisdom and the insights they stimulate will work well for us all—now and in the years to come.

When I talked about hope to the graduating clergy of AJRCA in the spring of 2022, the response to my teaching was very positive. Dr. Mel Gottlieb, then the longtime President of the

AJRCA, commented that for him, hope means *action*. For me, this has also been true throughout my life. This is why Dr. Eugene B. Borowitz stresses the importance of empowerment. Yet the time for action, whether individual or communal, requires careful thought and strategic planning. So we might say that action is the corollary to hope that lifts us out of despair.

However, as biblical history teaches us, sometimes there is no time to think. The response must be immediate. And then we have to act instinctively, with trust in our Creator. Just as the first man to step in the waters of the Reed Sea did when Moses exhorted the Hebrews fleeing the Pharaoh's wrath to do so. In an act of faith, when others hesitated to jump into these unknown waters, his relative, Nachshon,[146] brother-in-law of Aaron, the high priest, did so, and by his heroic example giving courage to the rest to follow.

In today's parlance, we would call them refugees, these Hebrews, these *Ivris*, fleeing for safety from people who want to annihilate them, a biblical precursor for refugees in similar circumstances through the centuries—and, indeed, a parallel to our present time.

And because I believe that hope itself is a miracle—not wishful thinking, not an illusion, but a realizable vision—I am asking you, dear reader, to close your eyes for a moment, to offer a silent prayer for the refugees of this world in this era in which we live, whose lives have been lost or unspeakably disrupted at home, and for those who face the task of remaking their lives as millions of strangers in new lands. As history sadly repeats itself, please pray silently in your own words for better times to come. Help unlock the door of hope for those who need a sustaining belief to move forward. They are also ours. Help them to believe that miracles are what you make of them.

* * * *

Faith—the flame that keeps hope alive

Faith is the flame that keeps hope alive. The Jewish religion is the story of that faith, that hope. The ancient rabbis of the Talmud understood that the ability to maintain hope in the direst of circumstances helped the Jewish people to survive. Without maintaining hope, the Jewish people would not have survived as *Am Yisrael*, the Jewish people. Against the historic background of the destruction of the Temple, the death of large numbers of Jews through catastrophic revolt, and the loss of many others to exile, the rabbis tried to pinpoint the specific point at which one abandons or does not abandon hope. With its usual precision, the Talmud tries to answer that question. The rabbis even considered whether one could abandon hope retroactively.

Can hope ever be abandoned?

There is a Hebrew name for the abandonment of hope. It is called *ye'ush.* Various fascinating perspectives—psychological, theological, ethical, and legal—can all be applied to *ye'ush.* It also has a related concept, *ye'ush shelo medat* (abandoning hope without knowing it—in other words, subconsciously giving up hope). Both concepts appear in a very small tractate of the Talmud called *Bava Metzia.*[147]

What do these ideas really mean? *Can one ever abandon hope?* If so, under what circumstances? Does it mean, as Aviva Gottlieb Zornberg suggested, that one then sinks into deep despair? How does one turn the coin of despair over to the other side and become hopeful once again? The story of Mrs. Mandelbaum offers some clues.

The Hope of Mrs. Mandelbaum[148]

When I was a young woman in Montreal, Canada, our family used the dressmaking services of Mrs. Mandelbaum, a middle-aged Holocaust survivor. We would go to her immaculate apartment, where her newly bought furniture was protected with plastic covers, and where she lived with her husband and son. There our dressmaker spent a great deal of time on her knees on the hardwood floor, as she pinned up the hemlines of her affluent clients.

When her only son reached Bar Mitzvah age, Mrs. Mandelbaum invited all her customers and sent out invitations to fellow survivors of the horrific concentration camp experience they had somehow managed to live through to liberation. She also invited some survivors she had encountered in the Displaced Persons camp after World War II. That was where she met her husband and conceived her son. From the D.P. camp, the Mandelbaums managed to get sponsorship to Canada, where we, the Bar Mitzvah invitees, were now their only "family." And everyone who was invited came.

The American-born guests/customers were amazed at the lavishness of the Bar Mitzvah. How could a woman of such limited means, someone they saw mainly down on her knees, afford such an elaborate celebration? Mrs. Mandelbaum knew how. She had saved every cent of her dressmaking money for more than five years to make hosting this occasion possible.

But her fellow survivors, the ones who flew in from the U.S., from South America, from Australia, from Israel—from wherever they had found refuge after the war—were not surprised. They understood that it was the hope that one day she would have a son who would provide continuity to the Jewish people through his Bar Mitzvah commitment that kept her alive in the concentration camp. The survivor-guests had promised one another that, if they made it through the war, they would be the witnesses to the celebration.

No matter where life took them, they would serve as one another's family. They had shared a common flame of hope, and now it had come to fruition.

It was a wonderful celebration. And after the Bar Mitzvah, Mrs. Mandelbaum got up from her knees. She did not have to pin up other people's dresses anymore.

* * * *

Afterthoughts

Mrs. Mandelbaum did not give up hope. At no time, did she enter a state of *ye'ush*, of hopelessness. As Viktor Frankl wrote in his famous book, *Man's Search for Meaning*, hope was an essential quality in keeping many survivors alive.[149] By focusing on serving as witnesses to the Holocaust or by being present at just such a future celebration as the Bar Mitzvah of Mrs. Mandelbaum's son, some people were able to keep going and live to rebuild a future. Mrs. Mandelbaum's story is about someone who refused to give up hope in a horrific situation. Her refusal in this instance concerned people.

By contrast, a second small section of the Talmud called *Bava Metzia* deals not with life and death issues—although it can be extended to those ideas. Rather, this section is about the maintenance or loss of hope in regard to inanimate objects—the loss of property, for example. In fact, the concept of what, in modern parlance, might be called "finders-keepers, losers-weepers" concerns the Talmud greatly: Someone who finds a lost object can keep it only when the owner has given up all hope of recovery, when the owner has abandoned hope and made it "ownerless." This is called *ye'ush shelo medat*.

Added to this issue of either maintaining or giving up hope of recovery of that property— that object, that thing— the Talmud raises another question: In what circumstances and at what point, does one abandon hope? At what point does one despair of retrieving lost property?

Then a further question is raised: Can one abandon hope without knowing it? Or can the finder act as if this has occurred and thus treat the object as ownerless? And even further, can *ye'ush* be retroactive? In other words, even if we were unaware of the loss of property at the time it happened—*if we had known* facts that were revealed only later—could it be treated *as if* we would have given up hope at the time the property was lost?

When something happens to us personally, we soon find out. Let me share with you another true story, this time about something that happened to me, about personal property that was lost.[150] Like many rabbinic *aggadot*, my real-life story, "Moving On?" makes its point in a rambling, round-about way. The reader or listener does not know where the story is going until it gets there. My story also makes much use of repetition and, especially, humor, two characteristics of rabbinic stories.[151]

* * * *

Moving On?[152]

It was Rosh Hashanah, the Jewish New Year. After I finished stuffing a turkey for a holiday celebration and, with a sigh of satisfaction, had put it in the oven for about twenty minutes per pound at 400 degrees *Fahrenheit*, and with a nicely folded foil tent over it, I began to tidy up the kitchen. That was when I noticed that my beautiful, emerald-cut diamond was missing from the ring that had marked my engagement, a ring, that together with my matching wedding band, I never, ever took off. I had been wearing it for many years. The engagement ring was still on my finger all right, but there was a big, gaping hole in the center where four prongs had formerly held the lovely gem.

My diamond was lost! No, I did not enter into a state of *ye'ush*, not at the beginning. I still hoped; no way would I abandon hope. I searched all over the kitchen, in every nook and cranny of the floor, the counters, for my diamond. Not too easy to find a clear diamond on a white tile floor or white counters (white, European kitchens were in vogue then), but ... no diamond! I searched and washed all the dishes in the sink. Nothing had been put in the dishwasher yet, so maybe...no, no diamond. "Oh no," I cried. "The turkey!"

Releasing a keening sound of something that was not yet resignation, that still had a note of hope in it, I removed the turkey from the oven, and, bit by bit, removed what would have been a delicious stuffing from the turkey, examined it with a magnifying glass, kneaded each morsel carefully between my fingers. No diamond was to be found. Next, as I peered into the now empty cavity of that turkey and poked and prodded its insides (fortunately it had been deceased for some time), the sinews glistened back at me as if they were laughing. After all, the turkey had been cooking in a pre-heated oven for twenty minutes. It dripped a little here and there.

It was at this point that I began to cry. I entered a state of resignation, a state of *ye'ush*, but I did have the presence of mind to report the loss to the insurance company. "My diamond is gone," I sobbed. At least some of the economic value, if not the sentimental value, was recoverable. And it did not take too much effort to report an insured loss. Now, if I had known that the diamond could not be found, that the loss was irrevocable despite all my effort, at the time the loss occurred, would I have entered a state of retroactive *ye'ush* immediately—that is *ye'ush* without knowing it, *ye'ush shelo medat*? It would have saved me a lot of searching time!

However, *my story is not finished*. When I finally served the turkey to my guests at a beautifully laid table that night, there it was, my diamond, floating in the gravy, as several of my guests pointed to it with astonishment. Thank goodness nobody had swallowed it! And yes, the diamond was undamaged. Diamonds, as you probably know, can survive high heat.

Yes, I had abandoned hope prematurely! Can we ever know, I reflect now, the precise time at which hope should be abandoned? Is there a time when we should give up hope and say, "Move on now! Collect the insurance money! Forget the sentimental value! Replace the diamond!"

But that is not the end of the story. Some years later, my diamond ring, this same diamond ring was stolen. A thief, a *ganaf,* broke into my house by stealth and stole all my jewelry, including this ring. And, *oy vay,* this time I no longer had jewelry insurance. It was too expensive! Since I was living in a large, metropolitan centre where one diamond is like another diamond, I realized that I probably would not recover it. Even before the police advised me that it was unlikely I would recover the ring, that the thief would have fenced it or shipped it to another country before I had even discovered the loss. There were no identifying marks because the ring was not engraved with an inscription or initials, and, in any case, the thief would likely have taken the diamond out of the ring for resale. So this time, my *ye'ush* was not in vain. I had to abandon hope for real.

But since, as the police said, it was already too late to retrieve my loss before I even discovered it was missing, was this not also *ye'ush shelo medat—ye'ush* without knowing it? In other words, if I had known, would I have given up hope of recovering it from the moment it was stolen, even before I actually knew it was stolen?

It's still not the end of this story. After I set this seemingly cyclical tale of loss and recovery and loss down on paper, I had a sudden urge to put "recovery"—hope—back into the picture when a recurring advertisement in a very reputable magazine caught my attention. Here a company reachable on the Internet was advertising gem-quality diamonds that looked very much like the one I had lost and found and lost again. Only these diamonds were not extracted from deep in the ground through the grime and sweat of miners working in unspeakably treacherous conditions that have been the subject matter of contemporary movies. These advertised diamonds were cooked in a scientific lab, and, yes, they had all the properties of natural diamonds found in the ground—but with one very important difference: They were flawless, a quality almost impossible for natural diamonds to attain. And, yes, these synthetic diamonds had another favorable attribute: The price was miniscule in comparison to what a "real" diamond would cost.

The temptation was too great to resist. I selected my ring (platinum-fused silver), with the large emerald-cut center stone surrounded by smaller baguettes on the side, just like the ones my long-lost ring (solid platinum) had possessed. Again, there was a difference. This time the emerald-cut stone I chose was not a diamond; it was a synthetic emerald, proudly reflecting four karats of polished green, chemical properties in the sunlight.

It is a very beautiful ring but somewhat ostentatious, so I wear it rarely. When I do, however, it is unlikely that anyone would realize that this artful replacement for my lost jewel is synthetic. But *if* an unknowing thief should attempt to steal it from my jewelry box at any time in the future, that *ganaf* will have gained only an object of no significant value, not compared to the multiple lives that have been lost in mines over the centuries trying to dig out that sparkling "real thing"—like the one I formerly owned—from the ground.

* * * *

As mentioned earlier, Jewish tradition calls Jewish law (i.e., what the rabbis decided in their wisdom) the *halakha.* One does not have to practice Orthodoxy to appreciate its intricacies. Even for Reform Jews, who do not usually feel bound by the *halakha,* or for non-Jews who are studying law or ethics or philosophy, or religion, it can be edifying to study the wisdom encapsulated in some of the age-old issues. Even after two millennia, these tenets prove helpful in understanding contemporary situations.

The controversy as to whether one can impose a state of *ye'ush* retroactively is, one of the most famous disputes among the *Amoraim* in the Talmud. In fact, many rabbis get into the act in deciding whose opinion should prevail. However, it would not be the Talmud if everyone had agreed on these issues.

* * * *

CHAPTER 13

MIRACLES

ARE WHAT YOU MAKE OF THEM

THE BOY: A MIRACLE EMBRACED

WHY HURT, LITTLE TOOTH?

The Boy: A Miracle Embraced[153]

The miracle was that it took place at all. The miracle was that the Bar Mitzvah happened. That a thirteen-year-old boy who could not speak and could not hear was leading a congregation with glowing hands that spelled out the words of God from an open Torah.

The boy was born of a Jewish mother. His father was gentile and black. His mother did not want him; his father had disappeared. He was unadoptable. Probably it would have been difficult to place him, even if he had not been deaf and mute.

After a series of foster homes, he found a friend—a teacher at the school for the deaf and mute who became very fond of him. The teacher was to become his adoptive father. He was not married; he was not Jewish.

The teacher believed that the boy was entitled to his Jewish birthright. He had a right to learn about and be proud of his heritage. The miracle began. The new father contacted the rabbi of a Reform Temple, and instruction was arranged for the boy. He was to have a Bar Mitzvah, the sacred act which confers new Jewish manhood. He would pray with his hands before the Ark of the Covenant.

In order to accomplish what is an ordeal for any thirteen-year-old, let alone one who can neither speak nor hear, his adoptive father would study along with him. As finally the boy recited with his hands before the congregation, the father would speak the words. And because the language of the Torah is both poetic and archaic, special instruction in liturgical sign language would be needed.

The day finally arrived.

The congregation had responded three hundred strong to the rabbi's request for them to come as Bar Mitzvah guests. They were to be the boy's family. He had been outfitted in new clothes. His light skin, framed by a halo of black curly hair, glowed. The ritual candles shone brightly. The light of the open Ark was reflected in the breastplates of the Torah. The adoptive father—round-faced, bearded, and jolly—translated the language of the boy's hands into sound, into Hebrew.

For those sitting and watching as the boy's hands moved, it seemed as if there *were* words, as if we could almost hear the sound of his hands without his father's vocal translation. It was as if the boy's hands had set in motion a sound of joy so high that the vibration could be heard. It was as if, rocking back and forth to the newfound rhythm of truth in the Torah, the hands danced and then burst into exultant song: "Once I heard nothing, now I have the sound of God in my head. Once I had no one of my own. I was so lonely. Now I'll never be alone again."

I have been to so many Bar Mitzvahs; but on this night the character of what took place strengthened my belief in the enduring vitality of sacred rituals. They are our umbilical cord to an appreciation of the wonder of creation.

On this night that I will never forget, I believe that I witnessed a miracle. Here, standing before God, was a creature so challenged in life, yet brought to this beautiful moment through the loving kindness of an adoptive single man. It happened. The gentile father gave birth to the Jewish son.

The father did not speak his thoughts before the congregation, but they were, I thought, clearly written on his face. "We finished what God started, my son. I wanted you to believe so that, even when I am gone, you will have someone to trust. You were born with every strike against you, but tonight you have taken your rightful place in this world. For me, you are a miracle."

On that night the miracle was also that the witnesses to this birth, paying homage in sacred ritual, were themselves brought to life. In a kind of self-purification through the pain and joy of a young man-to-be, their own human spirit was ignited and reborn.

Rabbi Corinne Copnick

BAR MITZVAH

Thirteen year old
fingers freshly trace
the journey's path...

There are so many maps,
even the choice of cartography
itself inks a studied
selection, dear son, which
is art—how you follow it
simply skill, a technique.

Coming's the climax, testing
true manhood—directions
you'll dare at life's crossroads,
charting an original...
                —*Corinne Copnick*

Why Hurt, Little Tooth?

I'm going to tell you a true story about my father who was a Montreal dentist. I first told this story at a storytelling session, where one creative artist after another got up and told a story. We made them up. To relax. For fun. Because, after two days of workshopping, it was a time for sharing. And now I want to share my story with you.

At the storytelling session, just before my turn, a young student was telling a story about chickens, and the story preceding her story concerned the financially hard times we were experiencing in Canada in the early nineties. But only half of my mind listened to the students' tales. I was spinning my own reverie, the other part of my mind taking me back to the 1930s, to the "real" depression years. I was thinking about hard times, about chickens...about my father. He had so recently passed away.

The chickens I was remembering were the ones my father got in return for fillings in the jobless thirties. Then people asked, "Are you working?" instead of "Hello, how are you?" If you were working, you were obviously all right.

In that very real depression in 1936, the year I was born, my father was accepting not only chickens, but their offspring, eggs. He would receive a wide assortment of other small items (usually grown in people's back yards) bartered in return for dental work. His impoverished clients could not otherwise pay. My father had been providing food for his own little family in this way since 1933, the year he graduated in dentistry from McGill University.

He had actually been accepted into medicine, quite an achievement at a time when McGill accepted few Jews (the university had a quota), especially a poor boy like my father— who sat with his hands covering the elbow holes of his jacket.

My father, the son of a junk peddler, was the only one of eight children to make it to university. This he did by dint of several scholarships and also by holding three jobs at the same time. He peeled potatoes at the amusement park (late night shift), worked as a longshoreman on the docks (summer), and served as a guide on a Montreal tour bus (weekends).

But he couldn't accept his hard-won entry into medicine. In those days, a Canadian medical graduate had to do a two-year, unpaid hospital internship after graduation. This my father could never afford.

Instead he went into dentistry, which didn't require the roadblock internship. Although he was very proud of his surgical skills, what I remember most about my father was his compassion. Quite simply, he cared about his patients. He was the kind of dentist who brought morning tea and toast to a disabled patient he was worried about. Once I saw him give back money to a woman who paid him in handkerchief-wrapped quarters and dimes.

"You'll pay me when you have a little more money," he said softly. And when his patients didn't have any, they could bring him some bread or home-baked cake or garden peas—or a chicken.

We ate a lot of chicken. In those old-fashioned, caring, depression days, my father's office was in our home. In 1939 just before he voluntarily joined the army and went to war, I was just a little girl, but I remember playing with toys in my father's waiting room. I remember watching the stream of dental patients come with food and go out with fillings.

I remember the incredulous screams of joy that came from his office late one afternoon. My mother came running, and, for a long while after that, I heard sounds that, even to my little girl's ears that didn't know yet about miracles, signaled that something momentous was taking place here, in my father's office.

As I peeked in the doorway, I could see that an elderly woman who had come with a chicken was sitting in the dental chair. Tears were streaming down her cheeks, and they were also making joyful pathways down the face of the sister who stood, clutching her hand, beside her.

My father also stood, transfixed, his voice husky with emotion as he asked the elderly woman questions pertinent to this moment none of them would ever forget.

"You can see?" he asked in a hushed tone.

"I can see, I can see," the woman smiled through her tears. "Oh, dear God, I can see!"

Her sister had brought her to my father's dental office because she had been suffering from an agonizing toothache. To go to a dentist cost money she couldn't afford, and she had waited and waited until she couldn't bear the pain anymore. How could one little tooth hurt so much?

Finally, she came to my father. A kind man who would accept whatever she could spare, people said, and so she came with her little offering of food. She walked in, guided by her sister, because the elderly lady was blind. She had been unable to see anything, not anything at all, for several years.

As my father tried to alleviate this terrible ache with his dental arts, as he extracted the rotted, blackened tooth that poverty had kept in the old lady's mouth, she began to shriek her joyful disbelief. The tooth had been pressing on an optic nerve. For all those years the woman had been unable to see.

In my father's dental chair, as the tooth was removed, as the pressure on the nerve was taken away, she began to see. Oh, not all at once! At first she could only see shadowy glimpses, floating by in black and white. But in the days before color and clarity once again began to fill her world, she could see images—beautiful, long-lost images. She could see the shape of things to come. She could see that the world was a wondrous place where miracles can happen. And that there were people like my father in it.

It was not long after this incident that my father began to feed his family (now there was my sister) with a monthly check from the army. And in the newsletter printed by the Canadian army in Canada, and also in England where my father was stationed during World War II, a poem written by him appeared. I was only a little girl, but even I knew that the little tooth didn't hurt any more.

Rabbi Corinne Copnick

WHY HURT LITTLE TOOTH?[154]

Why hurt little tooth, thou art so pretty,
Embossed in gorgeous setting of limited space;
Pearly gem so strong yet so gingerly touchy,
Radiant smile enriched with such lovely grace?

Why hurt, little tooth, thou causes such commotion,
Ivory-like in beauty, the human face bedecks;
Nourished and innervated and in constant motion,
Simple central incisor to large molar complex?

Why hurt, little tooth, thou art so useful,
Poised so lofty in high domed arch;
Expression transmuted so sadly rueful,
Delicious, refined carbohydrate starch?

Why hurt, little tooth, thou art so contrary,
Expedient implement for food mastication;
In speech and in mood thou be most necessary,
Gear-like, with dynamic trituration?

Why hurt, little tooth, thou pampered, spoilt child.
Symmetrically patterned in even, continuous array;

Temper so fickle, when reason goes wild,

Perfection distorted in gloomy, painful dismay?

Why hurt, little tooth, thou causes such elation,

Your first eruption in the infant stage;

Can you not spare us this bitter aggravation,

Declining years of ever-changing phase?

       —Dr. Irving Copnick, z"l[155]

The Loss of the Protector[156]

As I helped feed my father in the dining room of the hospital for the aged where he was confined, I slowly became aware of an incessant refrain. It came from a nearby elderly female body, twisted and deformed. Professionally, a uniformed attendant continued spooning soup into the old lady's mouth. The soup dribbled down her chin while she chanted over and over again in Yiddish, *"Ich vil nor leben, ich vil nor leben!"* ("I want to go on living. I still want to live.")

The confused floor for the totally helpless. Despite all assurances, I was not prepared for my father's placement in surroundings where his companions were those who had lost their way in the world. My father had been a member of a healing profession. Now the healer could not be healed. I was not ready for this reality.

Nor was I prepared for the fact that my mother would be spending part of every day at the home-hospital and feeling guilty if she missed a morning. She had already tended him, confused and incontinent, for nine years by herself at home. She had been coming to the hospital every day for four years. She had exhausted herself and her financial resources. And so we moved the man that we both loved from this friendly, sectarian hospital to a larger government hospital—bright and airy—twenty miles away. My father had been an officer in the army, and this was a hospital for veterans.

When I walked through these halls lined with men occasionally saluting one another, reliving their days as heroes, remembering when they were healthy and went to war for their country, I could remember myself as a little girl, standing proudly beside my father, so handsome in his new Captain's uniform. Together we peered through the venetian blinds at the parade of soldiers smartly marching in unison several stories below.

My father….

I have come to accept that even when the loved one does not know you anymore, even when a gleam in the eye can no longer be evoked, there is still a breath of fresh air, a ray of sunshine, a taste of cool ice cream. These were the things my father could enjoy. Or the touch of my hand even if he didn't know it was mine. And when, just once, he tapped his foot in sudden response to a familiar song, I knew my father was, for those few seconds, alive in spirit for me.

In this more distant setting, we do not visit as often now. We feel the need to detach ourselves from the accumulation of what is now more than twenty years' witness to suffering, to remove ourselves from continually reliving the pain. But although he no longer knows us, he is still ours. Still a part of us. Neither can we abandon him.

"You understand, darling," my father had written to me during the war when I was just a little girl, "your father is a doctor and a soldier? I dream of you every night, and I pray to God to protect you while I am gone. I miss you terribly, but soon, very soon, I shall come home again."

I knew that I had brought my father to his last home. For that is the dread of placement—that it is final—a stepping stone to death. Only death will secure one's release, once admitted, from these walls. And you can't get out of death alive. That is what is so hard to face. That in placing someone you love, you must come to terms with your own mortality too.

What placing my father, with all its attendant sorrows, has given me that is positive, is a deeper understanding of the sanctity of life. That while the heart beats, there must be dignity, and that while the heart beats, there must be joy.

There is always compensation. When we placed my father here—his death in life—my mother began to live again. Who can know the mind of God?

* * * *

Afterthoughts

There is so much that we do not know about life and death in this world and the next. My father had not been able to utter a word for eleven years, nor to give any evidence that he heard the tender words with which my mother and I caressed him when we visited. Then, on a day that was earth-shaking for me, I told him that I was going to teach a course at McGill University (something I knew that he would prize), and for the next thirty seconds or so, my father burst into speech. He spoke to me in *Yiddish* (his first language as a young boy, but one with which he never addressed me), and the cascade of words told me how much he loved me, that I was the finest, the best. These words were the last my father, my earthly protector, ever spoke to me—or to anyone. They were his last words, a miraculous moment I will always remember.[157]

Death is a homecoming, according to Rabbi Abraham Joshua Heschel. In the final analysis, in the same way one prepares for life, one must prepare for death and depart with a sense of peace.

"The Jewish mystical tradition sees old age in a positive light," writes Rabbi A. J. Seltzer. "The more the powers of the body subside ... the stronger the spirit becomes."[158]

* * * *

Rabbi Corinne Copnick

CHAPTER 14

CHOOSE LIFE

CHOOSE LIFE
PIKUACH NEFESH (THE PRESERVATION OF LIFE)
YISKOR: HOPE AS A MIRACLE
BEDTIME PRAYER

Choose life...

by loving the Lord your God, heeding his commands,

and holding fast to Him.

For thereby you shall have life and shall long endure

upon the soil the Lord swore to your ancestors,

Abraham, Isaac, and Jacob,

to give to them

—Deuteronomy 30:19-20[159]

*I*n a world that has been so recently beset by disasters both natural and man-wrought, the biblical curses seem dangerously close to us at times: economic woes, earthquakes, famine, disease, oil spills, floods, tsunamis, nuclear contamination, revolution, chemical attacks on one's own people.

Some rabbis have asserted that the Holocaust experienced in the 20th century was God's punishment for the sins of the Jewish people for not keeping the terms of their holy covenant. I have to say straight out that I do not believe this Deuteronomistic approach to religion. I have seen too many instances of situations where bad things happen to good people, including my own father, for that to be true, something that the Book of Job amply illustrates.

We simply have to accept that our flesh and blood, earthly lives—all life, our lives, the lives of our parents—eventually come to an end. But that understanding does little to reduce the pain of watching an ailing parent, a beloved parent, decline and deteriorate when there is nothing more we can do to reverse the effects of nature. In many instances—if we are lucky—this is our first personal encounter with death, and it brings into question our own mortality. It is painful to lose our beloved protector, not the protector of theology or the supernatural one of fiction, but our own personal protector who participated in giving us life.

In the Jewish view, life is sanctified to the extent that a dying person is considered the same as a living person until he/she is actually dead. Nothing must be done to extinguish the life of a "flickering lamp," not even closing the person's eyes. The Talmud tells us that a sick person may not be moved, if by so doing it would hasten its death. While death must not be hastened, at the same time, obstacles to death need not be prevented so that, in effect, the process of death is prolonged. Thus it is permissible to remove an impediment to death but not to do something actively to *cause* the death. According to the *Shulchan Aruch*, if something is causing a delay in the exit of the soul, it is permitted to remove these obstacles to death.

Pikuach Nefesh, the Preservation of Life

For all Jewish denominations, and particularly the Orthodox, the Jewish precept of *Pikuach Nefesh*, the preservation of life, is very important. In Deuteronomy 30:19, as Rabbi Byron Sherwin reminds us, the Torah instructs us to "choose life." [160]

However, it is important to make distinctions, as in the case of a *goses*, someone in the process of dying, expected to live only another 72 hours (3 days). Jewish law prohibits doing anything to either prolong or hasten the life of a *goses*. In fact, Jewish law considers a *goses* to be "a living person in every respect, and, even in his/her last moments of life, he or she has to be treated according to this living status."[161]

A terminally ill person not yet in the process of dying is called a *terefah* (in a different category from a *goses*). I was rather shocked, in fact, when I first learned that, in Jewish law, a *terefah* is considered as a person already dead. Personally, I consider this classification premature in an age when new medical procedures and medications are always just around the corner.

However, In the opinion of Rabbi Eliot Dorff, an esteemed Conservative Rabbi, "the objective of medical care is to act for the patient's benefit. Consequently, the pain of the patient can prevent doctors to continue aggressive treatment when there is no reasonable chance of recovering from a terminal illness."[162]

Similarly, if someone is dying in great pain, we don't have to pray for that person's recovery but rather to pray that the person who will die in a few days (a *goses*) may expire quickly. This position raises a slippery slope of questions as to what constitutes medical interference.[163] In short, when do you say *dayenu* (enough)?

"[I]f the right to die is legitimized by statute," cautions Arthur D. Silk, "how long will it be before the *right* to die becomes the *duty* to die?"[164] A utilitarian approach, which Jews tend to reject but that is often discussed in our media, is that end of life cases are eating up medical dollars. In contrast, our Jewish tradition reveres (or at least is supposed to revere) the elder person. While a variety of perspectives including Jungian philosophy try to explain death in different terms, the Jewish mystical view is that both this world and the next world are real. In this sense, *death is a transition to the next life.*

* * * *

Yizkor: Hope as a Miracle

And may our good deeds live on in the way we are remembered! In the belief that hope itself is a miracle, I am including here the following excerpt from a moving, poetic book I edited in 1999 entitled *Violin of Stone*.[165] Ernest Raab,[166] who emerged from World War II to become a famous sculptor, originally wrote this book in his second language, French, to record his wartime experiences. Some years later, Jeremy Fox translated these fragments beautifully into English:

> "I had the strange feeling that I had become a solitary tree, lost in another world..... I let my tears flow as never before, for I had suddenly understood that my parents were no longer of this world, and that, from then on, I would be alone in the world....

> "The distant walls of my cavern echoed to my sobs. And one by one my tears struck the black stone with a dull thud. Their echo flew into the darkness and resounded in my ears like the tears of a broken violin, ever drier and more glacial.

"That night, Moshe-Yehudah,[167] son of Simon, seemed to me to become the sole survivor of humanity. Alone on earth and in the universe.

"I knew that my parents would have no burial and no tomb in their memory. So I decided to bury my father and mother in the deepest folds of my soul, so that they could find there what they could not find among men—their grave."[168]

For young Ernest, in that moment, hope evolved into action. His memories would eventually lead him to become an internationally famous sculptor, one who created a huge bronze memorial in Toronto to those who died in the Holocaust. With a tall candle inscribed with sculpted, spiraled names rising from its base, it could be lit at night to keep the memory of the Holy Community of *Kamarom* in Hungary, and the Jewish values its members had cherished, alive for the generations.

* * * *

I often wonder if the people we love ever really die for us. Do they ever really depart from us completely when their bones are interred? Some part of them surely remains inside of us—their offspring, their spouses or relatives, the confidences shared with close friends, the works they left behind, fueling our spirits as we remember them.

May that hope be realized in the World-to-Come—and in the world we presently inhabit too!

* * * *

When we were little girls, my sister and I recited a bedtime prayer every night with my mother. It began with a recitation of "God, make my little garden grow" (a beautifully rendered pictorial inscription, paired and hanging on my bedroom wall along with another illustrated inscription: "If I should die before I wake, I pray the Lord my soul to take.") My little sister and I would fall asleep, secure in the knowledge we were protected, even if our earthly father was overseas in England.

A few years later, with my father safely home again, we would add to our bedtime prayers the *Shema*, a statement of faith that has resonated with the Jewish people throughout the centuries.

> *Sh'ma Yisrael,*
> *Adonai Eloheinu,*
> *Adonai Echad!*
> Hear, O Israel, *Adonai* is our God, *Adonai* is One![169]

Rabbi Corinne Copnick

So this prayer has been inscribed in my heart from childhood until today when I am an elderly lady, close now in years to my eventual eternal resting place.

And now, each morning, as I awaken to this beautiful world, our planetary home in what I have come to think of, in today's parlance, as the *meta* universe, I chant softly another powerful prayer (given new importance to me with the advancement of age), in daily gratitude for the experience of a lifetime:

> *Modah ani l'fanecha,*
>
> *Melech Chai v'Kayam,*
>
> *She'hechzarta bee*
>
> *Nishmati B'chemla*
>
> *Raba Emunatecha.*
>
> I thank you, living and enduring King,
>
> for You have graciously returned
>
> my soul within me
>
> Great is Your faithfulness.[170]

CHAPTER 15

THE LAST CHAPTER: THERE IS NO END

HOPE AS A MITZVAH

HOPE AS A MIRACLE: CREATION

HAIL STORM (POEM)

MY PRECIOUS LINKS

THE MOMENTUM OF HOPE

"Be fruitful and Multiply...."(Genesis 1:28)

"You shall be as a tree planted beside streams of water, which brings forth its fruit in its season. Its leaves do not wilt; and whatever it does prospers."(Psalm 1:3)

Hope As A Mitzvah

*"I*t is precisely the capacity to perform miracles that defines the 'man of God,'" writes Jon D. Levenson in the *Resurrection and the Restoration of Israel: The Ultimate Victory of the God of Life,* "and it is by the miracles of God that the ever-dying, ever-reviving people of Israel lives."[171] It is this concept of hope that is a foretaste of the *sever* of the Messianic era.

Jon Levenson's views resonate within me every single day. However, while there is a strong spiritual emphasis in *Miracles Are What You Make of Them,* the spotlight here is primarily on hope in this world that we inhabit, one that, in our various circumstances and time in history, we will continue to teach our children and grandchildren to maintain and expand for many generations-to-come. In the year 2023 C.E., that is my understanding of the World-to-Come.

In this way, as the esteemed Rabbi David Woznica teaches, hope becomes a *mitzvah*, one that can grow into a sustaining flame, both for the next generation and the many generations beyond.[172] As we honor those who have departed from this life—by maintaining and improving upon their values in a present that has already become the future—the mitzvah of hope becomes the miracle of new life.

Hope as a Miracle: Creation

Often I ask myself these questions that rabbis routinely encounter—and that I have touched on in an earlier chapter: In this day and age, does Jewish hope extend to the realm of life after death? When we leave our fleshly bodies, what happens to our souls? Do we return to our maker in spiritual form? Just as water exists in many forms, do we also assume other forms, go to another world? Does our energy, what is left, rejoin *Ein* Sof? Or do we simply die in peace, content that the name we have left behind is a good one?[173]

* * * *

Contemporary scientists, like Dr. Bruce H. Lipton, an eminent epigeneticist[174] (and internationally esteemed as a genius cell biologist who pairs science with spirit), have been posing similar questions too. As human beings, we are more than our DNA, he claims. Our cells are receptors, drawing in the environment as well. Lipton offers the analogy of the human body as a television set:[175]

Suppose the human body is like a television set, he proposes, and I am the image on the television screen you are watching. Does my image "die" because the receptor (the television set) showing my image has a blow-out? Unlikely, he reasons, because if you plug in a different television set and tune it to the station you were watching, my image—originally received via a broadcast from the environment—will still be there, available to be downloaded by the replacement image. In other words, "my identity, my 'self,' exists in the environment whether my body is here or not," Lipton explains. "When my physical body (the TV receptor) dies, the broadcast (an environmental signal) is still present."[176] Continuing this television analogy, Lipton reminds us that, "as compositors," we humans mirror the universe.[177]

Through this technologically-inspired image, Dr. Lipton is offering hope in the World-to-Come for people who are facing death.[178] From a more intense spiritual viewpoint, many rabbinic stories address this same issue of hope, but from different perspectives, in this world as well as the next. The pervading hope is that each succeeding generation will be good people, true to the Covenant, fulfilling the commandments, making the world a better place. In that continuity lies our Jewish hope. And that is why I am writing this book.

Certainly, in a universe where earthlings currently hope to inhabit other planets, there is much to discover about the intricacies of Creation. If we look back to the beginning of Creation, the Divine injunction to human beings (in the form of Adam, the first man), is to be stewards of the earth, protecting the plants and animals, and enabling all of God's created beings to be fruitful and multiply. As a rabbi, I think of both human and animal reproduction issues as a route to lead us back, metaphorically speaking, to a second chance—an opportunity to reenter and refresh the garden of Eden. We certainly failed on our first attempt. Hopefully, we will do better this next time.

As the late Rabbi Jonathan Sacks wrote, "Hope is a human virtue, but one with religious underpinnings."[179] There is certainly a strong keynote of spirituality underlying contemporary environmental issues.

The initial command to be fruitful was, in fact, given to the animals while Adam, the first human was given the privilege of naming them. Then the same Torah commandment was given to the first created human beings, Adam and Eve, to also be fruitful and multiply: *p'ru urvu.* (Genesis 1:28).

God blessed them and God said to them, "Be fertile and increase, fill the earth and master it; and rule the fish of the sea, the birds of the sky, and all the living things that creep on earth." (Genesis 1:1-28).[180] That is how the first humans were commanded to be the stewards of the earth.

* * * *

Recently, I came across an excellent book on this subject called *Eco Bible,*[181] which has excited considerable interest. Two rabbis, Yonatan Neril and Leo Dee, who both served as contributing writers, present views very much in line with my thinking. They explain that the purpose of *Eco Bible*, which covers the five books of the Torah in two volumes, is to ensure that the Bible remains relevant for this generation and for those to come—and to influence people so that they will hold "values above expanding our own standard of living."[182]

As I see it, for many people, especially the younger generations, the word "sustainability" is already integrated into their thinking. Putting it into action in their daily lives requires a deeper commitment. Even though most of us express the urgent need for clean air, land, and water, and already have begun to feel the impact of climate change around the world—*and now where we live*—we are reluctant to make the necessary alterations to our way of life. This is true of governments, locally, nationally, and globally too, but even the best intentions are often superseded by commercial interests.

Those of us who are guided by the moral and ethical teachings of the Bible already know that, starting with the very first words "When God began to create the heaven and earth" (or, as earlier versions translated the Hebrew, "In the beginning God created...."), humans were instructed in the very first pages of

Genesis to take care of our planet and the living beings that inhabit it. But we should not forget that after six exhausting days of creation, God's job was done, and it was good. *Tov.* As God then informed us, the rest was then up to us, we humans. We were given the task of being the planet Earth's stewards, of taking care of what God had already brought into being, its plants and its animals.

As the human conservators of the animals, for example, we must not only take care of them, but we must also show them compassion. Animals must also be allowed to rest on the Sabbath. Furthermore, we must allow the land to rest too. The Jewish teaching of *Shmita* instructs us to let the land lie fallow every seventh year to restore its nutrients. (We are also advised to work hard and prepare doubly in the sixth year so that people will have stored food supplies in the fallow year.)

These concerns were later amplified in the *Mishnah* (the first part of the Talmud, written in Hebrew) as well. When I began my rabbinical studies, I was introduced for the first time to this body of legal opinions compiled in the first couple of centuries C.E. by the Tannaitic rabbis. The *Gemara* (which means "Completion") was written in Aramaic by the Amoriam, rabbis who followed over the following two or three centuries C.E., and editors eventually produced both the earlier *Jerusalem (Palestine) Talmud* and later the famous, more precise *Babylonian Talmud* (circa 5th century C.E.).

Rabbi Corinne Copnick

As part of their organization of the vast commentary, the editors divided the 68 tractates of the *Mishnah* into six sections. One section was called *Zeraim* ("Seeds"); it dealt in a surprisingly modern way with the agricultural needs of the biblical land of Israel and its people. After all, the early Israelites followed an agrarian way of life.

I was so intrigued with *Zeraim* that, although it is lengthy, I read it (in English translation) straight through like a novel. And I learned a lot. Did you know, for example, that it is not a good idea to mix crops in the same field? Why? Because the roots might mingle. Better to plant a row of onions between the crops. Why? Because the roots of onions grow straight down, and so the roots will be kept separate. There were many other practical suggestions. *Zeraim* is *gung-ho* on ecology.

We are also reminded in a much-quoted *Midrash* (a biblical elaboration) from *Kohelet Rabbah* (also known as *Ecclesiastes Rabbah*) that it our job as humans to take good care of the world: "God says to Adam, 'Be careful not to despoil or destroy my world—for if you do, there will be nobody after you to repair it.'"[183]

It's a scary thought. So we humans need to hustle and take care of our only world. Now. In this 21st century, it's called "sustainability," but our biblical literature has educated us in this regard for thousands of years. A passage in Deuteronomy, for example, cautions us to protect our fruit trees, even in time of war, something to think about seriously as television screens portray the devastation taking place in far-off places (at this writing, Ukraine, for example) on a daily basis. Living in peaceful southern California, with a garden full of beautiful fruit trees (orange, lemon, lime, and small apples—our next-door neighbors have figs), I cannot help but read the following passage from Deuteronomy with apprehension:

> "When in your war against a city, you have to besiege it for a long time in order to capture it, you must not destroy its [fruit] trees, wielding the ax against them. You may eat of them, but you must not cut them down.
>
> "Are the trees of the field human to withdraw before you into the besieged city? Only trees that you know do not yield food may be destroyed." (Deut. 20:19).[184]

Finally, the biblical hope is that each succeeding generation will be good people, true to the covenant, fulfilling the commandments, making the world a better place. In that continuity lies our Jewish hope.

I must confess that sometimes, when I watch late night or early morning reports, and especially images, of far-off wars and domestic aggression on television, I cannot help but experience bleak thoughts and memories of other times that attach to old age.

Rabbi Corinne Copnick

And yes, I worry for the current generation who have just entered new adulthood. I worry for my grandchildren. Will they, like earlier generations, be called to arms to protect their country?

HAIL STORM[185]

Today's bold headlines, honed in
humanity's most primal image,
permeate this peaceful retreat,
stratify the morning mist with
conflict's ominous shadow,
blaspheme this sacred rock.

Here, amidst primeval peaks, a
poet's prescient sorrow
waters the pure, thin air, and,
frozen, trembling,
shudders the perceptive earth in
persistent, icy warning.

Here shades of ancient strife
hover over full-grown children of
freedom, sharing transitory
pleasures while war portends,
unaware destruction beckons
a new generation, once again
dreamy-eyed and multi-hued,
to become its bride and groom.

—*Corinne Copnick*

So I am heartened when I re-read Rabbi Naomi Levy's little gem of a book, *Hope Will Find You*. Rabbi Levy offers this musing: "One of my favorite blessings in all of the rabbinic writings is, 'May you see your world in your lifetime.' I think it means," she writes, "may you experience the bliss of the World-to-Come in this world."[186] Yes, God's blessings are here to enjoy while we are alive.

And then, a joyful announcement of a long-awaited scientific advance toward the end of 2022, just before Hanukkah and Christmas, reinforces for me that the World-to-Come, in effect, is already on the way:

Reproducing The Power of the Sun?

Just for a moment, put your dark glasses on and imagine reproducing the power of the sun in a laboratory! Scientists at the Lawrence Livermore National Laboratory in California have recently done it! They have achieved a long-hoped for nuclear fusion breakthrough: how to create clean energy. For the first time, they have been able to reproduce the powers of the sun—in a laboratory.[187] And they have been able to do that, also for the first time, by creating more energy than it takes to reproduce the new energy. This accomplishment is indeed, in the words of lead writer Kenneth Chung, "a scientific milestone."[188] After all, fusion is the nuclear energy that can make the stars shine. It offers a huge improvement over existing nuclear power that splits uranium to produce energy. And as fossil fuels are burned, they create both pollution and greenhouse gases.

While past scientific experiments have *consumed* more energy than the fusion reactions *generated*, this time the new fusion experiments produced more energy, *finally reaching the ignition goal*. It has taken many years since construction of the National Ignition Facility started in 1997 to reach this goal. (Experiments began producing disappointing results in 2009. Little energy was actually produced.) Now there is good news, a breakthrough.[189]

To be sure, there have been dashed hopes throughout this lengthy process of eventual achievement, and there may be more disappointments along the way. Current predictions are that it still will be decades—at least 30 years, maybe 50—before nuclear fusion will begin to replace other forms of energy.

The great news, though, is that sometime later in this 21st century—the same century in which the polar caps are melting, affecting earth's climate and releasing strange viruses—something really hopeful will be happening. Something good, something clean, something big, it is projected to revolutionize the way energy is produced and utilized on this planet.

Maybe it will have arrived for my grandchildren in Generation Z, but more likely we'll finally have clean energy in the time of their children's or perhaps even their grandchildren's generation. We know now, at least, that it will assuredly happen in the World-to-Come.

> "For a tree has hope; if it is cut, it will again renew itself, and its shoots will never cease. If its roots are old in the earth, and its stump dies in the ground, at the scent of water, it will bud and produce branches like a sapling (Job 14: 7-9)[190].

What wonderful words to read in this year of the superbloom! We are also assured by the prophet Isaiah that, in time, a new shoot will always emerge from the stock of Jesse, the biblical King David's father. "A shoot shall grow out of the stump [trunk] of Jesse, A twig shall spout from his stock" (Isaiah 1:1). We need to remember, of course, that our concept of time and God's time do not always coincide.

It certainly does not, because that same James Webb telescope came up with another surprise recently. As reported once again in the *New York Times,*[191] it seems that the telescope was able to make out a very, very distant replica of our earth's own *milky way galaxy*. Probably our earth is the replica of that distant one because it's a lot older than we are. Much older. Also, we'll never get to visit there in our present lifetimes because it is more than a billion light years away.

Just the same, it's nice to know. Kind of comforting, isn't it? Could it be, as astronomy buffs speculate, that some future generation will set out to meet that galaxy—and a planet made from the same mold as ours? What a wonderful world this can be!

As a Vintage Original, I believe with all my heart that the World-to-Come is beginning right now—yes, here and now—with our newest, bright-eyed, forward-looking, educationally and ethically equipped generation.

* * * *

Hope as a Miracle: My Precious Links

With the understanding that the books I have written over the course of my lifetime—this is my sixth, as well as two plays and an attempt at a musical (the music was good)[192]—are a chain in my own spiritual evolution, I have invited both my granddaughters, Samantha and Rachel, as well as my grandson, Joshua, to contribute to this chapter. As their grandmother, I consider them part of my own evolution too, precious links in my personal chain of being, and I deeply hope that I am part of theirs.

All three are all members of Gen Z, the generation that will take us to the next step in the history of our world. And all three were deeply affected by the pandemic that closed their classes and required them to learn online—with little human contact with their teachers and their peers— which they did with great determination. They have endured, they have survived, and they have succeeded, with a deeply embedded desire to better a world in need of healing, along with its people. So this chapter had been written with Gen Z in particular in mind, and I am interested in their views. I may think of myself as a Vintage Original, but the future is theirs to shape.

I have asked each of them to contribute their suggestions to this chapter, and this is the prompt I provided at Joshua's request:

As a member of Generation Z, the Torch is passing to you. How do you envision the world you and your generation now hold in your hands, as did the generations before you? What are your hopes for this "World-to-Come"? How will YOU put these hopes into action.

Interview with Joshua

Joshua, the first-born of my grandchildren, possesses both an engaging personality and leadership qualities. Highly intelligent, he thinks deeply about our world. With a top-notch university degree in science behind him, he is now exploring "the creative side" of himself in Los Angeles: writing, experiencing film production, and deciding on his future direction. He has an entrepreneurial spirit. What may the future hold?

When I spoke to Joshua about writing a short essay for the closing chapter of this book to describe what he thinks the future may hold for Gen Z, like a true, newly graduated advocate of highly intelligent computer systems, he paused for a moment. Then he suggested that the best way to answer my question about the future was to make use of Artificial Intelligence (A.I.) itself—that is, to ask artificial intelligence to accumulate and digest specific information and compile the results in a format that would present likely outcomes for the Gen Z generation and beyond. "There's even a specific computer program that will do it for you, Grandma," he said. "I think it costs a few bucks. You ask the question, and it gives you the response."

Grandma's Comment: As of this moment, I'm still waiting for that super-intelligent computer to do the job. Meanwhile my equally super-intelligent grandson is still busy exploring the artistically creative side of himself. No computers involved yet.

And I'm glad. Serious concerns are growing now about the emergence of Artificial Intelligence (A.I.) Chatbots, which draw their information, as I understand it, from the Internet itself. This has both an upside and a downside because while they derive good information from the Net, they also draw the bad, and we run the risk that these bots may manipulate both to spread the kind of disinformation that can erode our society. One example, developed by a huge international tech company, is an amazingly intelligent Chatbot,[193] who will answer your questions within limits; unfortunately, its destructive dark shadow emerges if you engage or annoy the Chatbot too long. You won't want to meet that shadow, which assumes a different name from its counterpart.

Another example: The aggressive stance of a seemingly innocuous computer "game"—until it multiplies by invading other computers ruthlessly to achieve its materialistic goals: making more and more of its commonplace but necessary office product with the intention of capturing the world market.

The good side and the bad side—and how to maintain the balance of life with a guiding moral code—that's why mankind needed the biblical Ten Utterances in the first place, or so it seems to me. And why our Jewish folk literature has taught us to beware of *golems*—our technologically-devised superheroes, like the long-ago mechanical *golem* of Prague[194]—first considered a protective wonder by the persecuted Jews—until it ran amok, killing thousands of people, as its destructive side gained control.

Through the centuries, despite catastrophic occurrences, and despite our human limitations, we have always needed people to rebuild and to uphold the moral balance in this world. With destructive events still going on in this world as I write these words, it looks like we still need intelligent and courageous human beings (I.C.H.B., also known as ICHB) to protect and preserve our planet, so help us God, perhaps more than ever. A little assist from A.I. (as long as we are able to keep it within bounds as it develops) can help too.

* * * *

Interview with Samantha

My grand-daughter, Samantha (known to her friends as Sam and to me as Samee), is very close to my heart. She is a proud graduate of the University of California at Santa Barbara, with a double major in environmental studies and sociology. At graduation, she was awarded a special honor for achievement in environmental issues. Like Joshua, she is considering her future path during a gap year. Her first decision was to accept the opportunity of a Birthright trip to Israel, where, along with visiting fascinating historic sites, she explored the Galilee on an electric bike. She also undertook to have a second *Bat Mitzvah* at the Western (previously "Wailing") Wall, which she found very meaningful. When Samantha slipped a written prayer to God into a crevice of the wall, like thousands and thousands of other visitors over time, she became a part of Judaic history.

On her return to the U.S., she began a seven-month fellowship with AmeriCorps, concentrating on environmental justice and leading an informational (and fun-filled!) "new energy" event in a large and beautiful outdoor venue. As an avid rock climber, Samantha also managed to visit several U.S. national parks this summer. She was thrilled to be accepted into a top-notch, pioneering Master of Architecture degree in Canada. A professional degree, it emphasizes both sustainability and creativity. Her studies begin in September, 2023. Our following short interview outlines some of Samantha's own hopes for the future of our planet.

My question to Samantha was this: "What environmental conditions does our global society need to create to allow reproduction (humans and animals) to return to sustainable proportions?"

Samantha said that she is certainly aware that there is an overall world-wide fertility crisis—both among animals, including sea animals, and human beings. She believes, though, that we can't simply pin this situation solely on the fact that people are taking birth control pills or other means to delay pregnancy or waiting too long to raise a family. Rather, she points to chemicals and microplastics as a major cause.

"So what's the environmental factor creating these 21st century problems," I asked her. "Something is permeating the waters," she believes. In other words, substances like microplastics are disrupting the environment. She informed me that there is actually a growing movement of people trying to get pregnant by eradicating plastics and hormone disrupters from their lives as much as possible.

"You know, Grandma," she said, "throughout human history there have been natural disasters that have caused mass extinction. We are currently in the sixth mass extinction. But this time, it's by our own hand, and other animals who are not human are feeling the brunt of it." Then, as an afterthought, she remarked thoughtfully, "It's not as if we need more people now; the world is severely overpopulated."

"What do you think has caused this situation?" I asked my very smart granddaughter. She attributed this phenomenon to the desire to sustain a strong imperialistic and capitalistic system, to the need to make more and more profit.

"So what should we be doing, Samantha? What's the solution to these problems?"

"We need unbiased education," she replied. "Right now we have a system that encourages misguided, biased education in order to sell products. Since we can't control anyone to do our bidding, we need to lead by example. We can't force anyone."

"So would you say that the solution is education and example?"

"Yes," Samantha responded, and then she added, "but the world's not ours. We live on it, but we can't control the world. But we *can* do what humans can do. We are at the top of the food chain, but only because we have guns."

"I still believe humans are inherently good," I objected. "That's been my experience."

Samantha shook her head. "I am not so sure. Human beings are good when there is a mutualistic benefit. For example, look at the domestication of dogs and farm animals. There was a mutualistic benefit."

So after our conversation, I thought for a while. And then my idealistic bright light went on. After all, I have 87 years of living experience. "Maybe what the world needs now are *mutualistic benefits*. Yes, with unbiased education and good example and mutualistic benefits, I think there's good reason to hope in the 21st century."

So once again, *Mah tovu?* What is good?

* * * *

Rachel's poem

My younger grand-daughter, Rachel, decided that, rather than an essay or an interview, she would like to contribute a poem to the future. Rachel's cup of talent runneth over and then some. She is awesomely multi-talented in the arts, especially in music, and she has a glorious voice and range. With high school graduation accomplished, she is concentrating on her music now, studying and composing in Los Angeles, and open to the direction(s) in which it will take her. Rachel is also a very caring person. Here is her accolade to the future:

THE MOMENTUM OF HOPE[195]

hope is love

empathy

compassion

fear

hope sparks flames

and borrows our breath

hope is complex

that's what we're taught

yet

there is so much more...

fear blinds us

ignorance denies us

terraforms the fields of change

of hope

but

change is not something to fear

hope is never giving up hope

the moment it's lost

that momentum's energy

lessens—even disappears

hope cannot exist without itself

that's why it's so important to share it

I will be there for you

You will be there for me

hope is as easy as breathing

breathe it in

breathe it out

breathe it forth and repeat

with enough practice

it's that simple

hope guides us

to be better

to know better

to do better

together, we hope

a universal language

that's what brings change

and every change brings hope.

—*Rachel Spiegel-Brown*

As with all successive generations, Gen Z now inherits the role of Caretaker of our world. Our prayers are with you, in your youthful strength and idealism. In order to succeed, this has to be a collective trust. It will take all of us, together, to succeed. And pretty soon the Alpha generation (as we begin the alphabet all over again) will be joining the humans on our planet too.

All of us, all over the world, together we can employ our individual strengths, and the wisdom of generations past, to help ourselves and our children (and continuing with our grandchildren, and those to come) to fulfill this sacred trust: Our World, the only world we have. Like the Talmud's elderly Honi the Circle Maker (*HaMe-agel*, a roofer by profession, who inscribed circles to interact with God),[196] he slept for seventy years. When he awoke, he found the world so different and peopled by generations who did not know him. Yet, in his mature wisdom, he continued to plant carob trees, which take 70 years to grow, for his descendants.

There is a lot to learn from the wisdom of our heritage. Taking this Talmudic example to heart, may each of us, using our education and strength and God-given talents, continue to plant and grow our ideas, along with our children, helping them branch out to become whatever they may be, even if they take seventy years and a lot of watering to grow to fruition—not for ourselves but for the next generation and the ones after that. And let us

Rabbi Corinne Copnick

continue to hope. Seeded with knowledge and inspiration—and watered with effort —hope is a gift to the future.

Miracles are what you make of them.

APPENDIX 1

GUIDE FOR BOOK CLUBS: QUESTIONS TO CONSIDER

WHAT DO YOU BELIEVE?

Discussion 1:

1. What kind of future is informed by the past?

2. What lessons do we learn from the present?

3. Is catastrophe necessarily the other side of hope?

4. Is optimism the same as hope?

5. Can we imagine a positive future, one informed by both the past and present and our own values?

Discussion 2:

1. Is it by God's miracles that the people of Israel live?

2. Is rational thinking also an essential tool in moving from despair to hope?

3. Do you believe that a sense of purpose keeps people alive?

4. Is it possible for an individual to hope alone—without any or minimal support?

5. To what extent do we change ourselves, and to what extent do we count on helping hands from others?

Discussion 3:

Do you believe that:

> 1. Human beings and the world we inhabit are in a continual state of becoming?
>
> 2. The possibility for change is always possible?
>
> 3. Both courage and persistence play a role in maintaining hope?
>
> 4. We have to be brave enough to dream—and to ACT on those dreams, sometimes against all odds?
>
> 5. What is most effective in inspiring and maintaining hope: Collective Support or Inner Strength?

Discussion 4:

> 1. When do our actions depend on the situation and the need?
>
> 2. Can a teenager born into Judaism, but converted to another religion by parents anxious to protect her from persecution, return to Judaism on a part-time basis when she is an adult?
>
> 3. If she still feels close to Judaism but brings up her children in her non-Jewish spouse's faith to maintain household peace, is she still a Jew?
>
> 4. Is she still a Jew if she feels most at home in Jewish cultural (but not synagogue) life, maintains Jewish

friends, and becomes involved in leadership positions in the Jewish community?

5. What does this person do as the end of life approaches if she still feels drawn to her birth religion?

Discussion 5:

1. Is redemption dependent fully on human choice and man's will to change?

2. Is it possible to construct a viable religious approach without the certainty of redemption?

3. To what degree can one accept uncertainty?

4. How does it intersect with hope?

5. How do we handle these tensions?

Discussion 6: Specifically for Gen Z

1. As a member of Generation Z, the Torch is passing to you. How do you feel about that?

2. How do you envision the world you and your generation now hold in your hands, as did the generation before you?

3. What are your hopes for this "World-to-Come"?

4. How would YOU put these hopes into action?

5. Make a do-able plan.

APPENDIX 2

Certificate gifted to Corinne and Albert Spiegel in 1958. Mary and Harry, Albert's parents, purchased 200 trees to be planted in Israel in the bridal pair's honor. In 2023, some 65 years later, deep in an Israeli forest, these trees still flourish. (Photo J.Spiegel, ©Los Angeles, 2023.)

DECLARATION OF INDEPENDENCE OF THE STATE OF ISRAEL

"The Land of Israel was the birthplace of the Jewish people. Here their spiritual, religious, and national identity was formed. Here they achieved independence and created a culture of national and universal significance. Here they wrote and gave the Bible to the world.

"Exiled from Palestine, the Jewish people remained faithful to it in all the countries of their dispersion, never ceasing to pray and hope for their return and restoration of their national freedom.

"Impelled by this historic association, Jews strove, throughout the centuries, to go back to the land of their fathers and regain statehood. In recent decades, they returned in their masses. They reclaimed a wilderness, revived their language, built cities and villages, and established a vigorous and evergrowing community, with its own economic and cultural life. They sought peace, yet were ever prepared to defend themselves. They brought blessings of progress to all inhabitants of the country.

"In the year 1897 the first Zionist Congress, inspired by Theodor Herzl's vision of a Jewish State, proclaimed the right of the Jewish people to a national revival in their own country.

"This right was acknowledged by the Balfour Declaration of November 2, 1917, and reaffirmed by the Mandate of the League of Nations, which gave explicit international recognition to the historic connection of the Jewish people with Palestine and their right to reconstitute their National Home.

"The Nazi holocaust which engulfed millions of Jews in Europe proved anew the urgency of the reestablishment of the Jewish State, which would solve the problem of Jewish homelessness by opening the gates to all Jews and lifting the Jewish people to equality in the family of nations.

"Survivors of the European catastrophe as well as Jews from other lands, claiming their right to a life of dignity, freedom and labor, and undeterred by hazards, hardships and obstacles, have tried unceasingly to enter Palestine.

"In the Second World War, the Jewish people in Palestine made a full contribution in the struggle of freedom-loving nations against the Nazi evil. The sacrifices of their soldiers and efforts of their workers gained them title to rank with the people who founded the United Nations. On November 29, 1947, the General Assembly of the United Nations adopted a resolution for reestablishment of an independent Jewish State in Palestine.

"This recognition by the United Nations of the right of the Jewish people to establish their independent state may not be revoked. It is, moreover, the self-

evident right of the Jewish people to be a nation, as all other nations, in its own sovereign state.

"Accordingly we, the members of the National Council, representing the Jewish people in Palestine and the Zionist movement of the world, met together in solemn assembly by virtue of the natural and historic right of the Jewish people and of the resolution of the General Assembly of the United Nations, hereby proclaim the establishment of the Jewish State in Palestine, to be called Israel.

"We hereby declare that, as from the termination of the Mandate, at midnight, this night of the 14th to 15th of May, 1948, and until the setting up of duly elected bodies of the State, in accordance with a Constitution to be drawn up by a Constituted Assembly, not later than the first day of October, 1948, the present National Council shall act as the Provisional State council, and, its executive organ, the National Administration, shall constitute the Provisional Government of the State of Israel.

"The State of Israel will promote the development of the country for the benefit of all its inhabitants; will be based on precepts of liberty, justice and peace taught by the Hebrew prophets; will uphold the full

social and political equality of all its citizens without distinction of race, creed, or sex; will guarantee full freedom of conscience, worship, education and culture; will safeguard the sanctity and inviolability of shrines and holy places of all religions; and will dedicate itself to the principles of the Charter of the United Nations.

"The State of Israel will be ready to cooperate with the organs and representatives of the United Nations in the implementation of the resolution of November 29, 1947, and will take steps to bring about an economic union over the whole of Palestine.

"We appeal to the United Nations to assist the Jewish people in the building of its state and admit Israel into the family of nations.

"In the midst of wanton aggression, we call upon the Arab inhabitants of the State of Israel to return to the ways of peace and play their part in the development of the state, with full and equal citizenship and due representation in all its bodies and institutions, provisional or permanent.

"We offer peace and amity to all neighboring states and their peoples, and invite them to cooperate with the independent Jewish nation for the common good

of all. The State of Israel is ready to contribute its full share to the peaceful progress and reconstitution of the Middle East. Our call goes out to the Jewish people all over the world to rally to our side in the task of immigration and development, and to stand by us in the great struggle for the fulfillment of the dream of generations—the redemption of Israel.

"With trust in Almighty God, we set our hands to this declaration at this session of the Provisional State Council in the city of Tel Aviv this Sabbath eve, the fifth day of Iyar, 5708, the fourteenth day of May, 1948."[197]

Three years after the conclusion of the Second World War (1939-1945), and after the United Nations mandated the new Jewish State, to be called Israel, this Declaration of Independence was signed in Tel Aviv on the fifth day of *Iyar*, 5708 (May 14, 1948). The next day, as is well known, five Arab armies attacked the newly established State of Israel with intent to destroy the fledgling State. They did not succeed.

ACKNOWLEDGMENTS

*M*iracles Are What You Make of Them, represents the culmination of so many positive influences during my lifetime. Since I was ordained as a rabbi in late life, I especially want to acknowledge the following "influencers" in respect to this, my sixth book.

It is more than 16 years since I began my studies at a rabbinic seminary, AJRCA, and a decade since I was ordained as a rabbi. The teachings of my former professors (now my rabbinic colleagues) at the pluralistic Academy for Jewish Religion in Los Angeles are integral to the creation of this book. So I offer heartfelt thanks to each and every one of these dedicated instructors for their grasp of intricate mystical concepts and ability to translate them into present day realities; for sublimating the sense of proximity to upper reaches into moving ritual; for bringing the loving teaching of the Hebrew language close, for instilling in me a love of the Talmud and other Judaic texts; for introducing me to the depth of the history and ideas of modern Jewish thought and of Comparative Religion, as well as the intricate history of Israel, past and present; for emphasizing that action should follow words; and for celebrating joy as well as mourning sorrow. Very special thanks to Dr. Joel Gereboff, who served as my rabbinic thesis director in 2014, and who wrote the beautiful Foreword to this book.

I would also like to offer deeply appreciative thanks and gratitude for the insightful opinions about hope from the "garden" (as I refer to it) of brilliant contemporary rabbis and distinguished academics, some of them colleagues, some whom I have never met, alluded to in these pages. The list is long: Rabbis Bradley Artson, Tal Becker, Elliot Dorff, Tamar Frankiel, Mel Gottlieb, Irving Greenberg, Avraham Greenstein, David Hartman, z"l, (whose Montreal services I attended many years before he moved to Israel); Joshua Heschel z"l, Maurice Lamm, Naomi Levy, Michael Marmur, Simon Noveck, Ephraim Oshry, z"l, Jonathan Sacks, z"l, J.B. Sacks, Joseph Telushkin, David J. Wolpe, David Woznica, and several world-famous writers, among them Torah scholar Aviva Zornberg, Victor Frankl (creator of "logotherapy"), and Elie Wiesel (biographer of the Holocaust), and deep thinkers David R. Blumenthal, Eugene B. Borenstein, Bruce H. Lipton, and Michael Oppenheim. Appreciation to Rabbi Laura Geller for her thoughtful focus on aging and to the *Jewish Journal of Greater Los Angeles/Tribe Media* for its excellent reportage on many fascinating Judaic issues. Thank you, thank you, thank you to the flowers of my rabbinic garden.

I am beyond grateful to *Sefaria.org* for making it possible to find biblical and other Jewish texts and their translations online with ease and to quote them in *"Miracles Are What You Make of Them."* Special thanks are due also to Rabbis Elliot Dorff, Joshua Ladon, and Bernard Steinberg, for the fact-filled and inspiring talks mentioned in these pages that they gave to the Board of Rabbis of Southern California. Also, I am emphatically in tune with the way Rabbis Yonatan Neril and Leo Dee have linked ecological concerns with biblical teachings, and to the Interfaith Center for Sustainable Development. The Shalom Hartman Institute and the lectures of its knowledgeable scholars have been an essential part of my online life, and to each one of them I give my sincere thanks. Thanks also to the American Jewish Committee for everything it does. Also my gratitude to Jonathan Sarna and Jerry Klinger, and to Cornell and Yale Universities for educating me about Mordecai Manuel Noah.

Special "kudos" also to some remarkable media coverage of scientific information: to CNN's Bill Nye, for example; to programs like CNN's "Big Ideas;" to knowledgeable CNN *Morning Brew* columnists and hosts; to the informative "Ted Talks;" and to famed Carl Sagan. Also to Nola Taylor for information about dark matter, and to writer Dara Horn for her innovative thoughts about antisemitism today in relation to the enormity of the Holocaust. Scientific reporting in the *NY Times* and the *Jerusalem Post* has been outstanding and thankfully made understandable to the layman by skillful reporters like Kenneth Chung and others too numerous to name.

A big thank you, too, to the members of *Beit Kulam*, a Judaic study group I founded shortly before I graduated as a rabbi. They have participated whole-heartedly in early readings of portions of *Miracles* as the book progressed.

And, as usual, thanks from the bottom of my heart to my wonderful family for their encouragement and participation. In fact, the creation of this book has turned into a family project. My amazing daughter, Janet Spiegel, undertook the formidable task of editing and formatting *Miracles Are What You Make of Them*, and otherwise getting it ready for the many aspects of publication. Thank you to my daughters, Laura and Susan, who read and copy-edited every single word of the manuscript with dedication and love, and to my talented daughter, Shelley, who gave excellent feedback throughout. Thanks also to my grown-up grandkids, Joshua, and Samantha, for sharing their Gen Z opinions, and for Rachel's beautiful poem. With creativity passing through the generations, an additional appreciation to my granddaughter, Samantha, who designed the book's working cover. Together we have indeed become a publishing "house."

I hope you have enjoyed *Miracles Are What You Make of Them*!

B'ahavah (love) to all my readers—at any age,

Rabbi Corinne Copnick

Rabbi Corinne Copnick

ABOUT RABBI CORINNE COPNICK

M.R.S. (Master of Rabbinic Studies, AJRCA),

M.A. (Developmental Drama, McGill),

B.A. (Honors English, McGill), C.M. (Canada Medal)

*W*hat an incredible journey! Born in Montreal, Quebec, Canada, Rabbi Corinne Copnick moved to Los Angeles, California in 2000 to be near her family. She is the proud mother of four wonderful daughters and three amazing grandchildren. She is also the grandmother of their Labradoodle, Penny.

With a rich background in the multidisciplinary arts (including as a CBC radio actress nationally in her Canadian youth, an art gallery owner in mid-life, and a writer throughout), she was ordained as a rabbi in 2015 at the age of seventy-nine. A former Governor of the Sandra Caplan Community *Bet Din* in L.A., she continues to serve as a *dayan* (judge in a rabbinic court for conversion). She still teaches the pluralistic educational group, *Beit Kulam*, she founded a decade ago.

After ordination, Rabbi Corinne, as she prefers to be called, served over the course of five years as a Guest Staff Rabbi on lengthy cruises around the world—the genesis of her 2020 book, *A Rabbi at Sea: A Unique Spiritual Journey*. During the Covid-19 pandemic, she was a virtual touring author for the Jewish Book Council Network.

Rabbi Corinne is the author of several other published books: *Embrace: A Love Story in Poetry* (bilingual poems in English and French); *Altar Pieces*, narrated and screened for five years on Canada's Vision TV, and for which she was honored with the Canadian Commemorative Medal (1992), awarded to those who have made a significant contribution to Canada; *How To Live Alone Until You Like It—And Then You Are Ready For Somebody Else*; and *Cryo Kid: Drawing a New Map* (2008), awarded finalist status in the 2009 National Indie Awards of Excellence. For several years, she was Entertainment Editor for *Jewish Life* and a regular columnist for *The Jewish Tribune* in Toronto. The recipient of various grants and scholarships, she was honored to serve as resident writer at the Banff Center for the Arts, Alberta (1990). Simultaneously, for fifteen years, she ran a successful writing and editing business. Her latest book *Miracles Are What You Make of Them*, examines hope from the culminated experience of an elderly person.

In her prior Montreal life, as owner of *Galerie La Magie de l'Art*, Rabbi Corinne created more than forty stellar exhibitions and cultural events. She designed a groundbreaking role-playing simulation on Canadian unity called *Future Directions*. An acclaimed play that she wrote for drug education purposes, *Metamorphose*, was featured at the Quebec Pavilion of Montreal's *Man and His*

World, as well as many other venues. In 1980, she was invited by the late Dr. Louis Miller (then National Psychiatrist of the Army in Israel) to give two workshops on the use of therapeutic theater for health professionals at the Jerusalem Theatre. In 1991, in cooperation with the Central Museum of Zagreb and the Jewish Museum in Belgrade, she organized an outstanding international exhibition, held in Toronto, of "Jewish Art Treasures from the former Yugoslavia."

She has also been an active volunteer throughout her life. In 1998, the National Council of Jewish Women (Montreal section) honored her work, with other past presidents, as a Woman of Distinction. She also served on the Boards of The Quebec Drama Festival, the St. James Literary Society, and Temple Emmanu-el Beth Shalom. In Toronto, she served on the Boards of Medina Theatre and the Jewish Theatre Committee of Greater Toronto. In California, she served on the Boards of West Coast Jewish Theatre and the Canadian Women's Club of Los Angeles. She also led a drama group (plays of societal interest) at Valley Beth Shalom synagogue for five years. Among her many affiliations she was a member of PEN International (Canada) and is a current member of the Board of Rabbis of Southern California.

Although Rabbi Copnick is *mostly* retired today, she was honored to lecture virtually in the Spring of 2023 as part of an Israeli educational program about the olive culture in the

Mediterranean Basin. Participants came from Israel, Albania, and Turkey.

MORE TITLES BY RABBI CORINNE COPNICK

Embrace/Etreinte, a unique, bilingual (English/French) collection of moving poems was written at a sensitive time in the history of Quebec. Today it is considered a rare book. Limited edition published by *Guy Maheux Edition Enr.*, Montreal, Quebec, 1981. ©Corinne Copnick Spiegel, Montreal, 1981; Los Angeles, 2023. All rights reserved. Cover is by acclaimed Canadian artist Ghitta Caiserman-Roth, R.C.A., inside photo art by Sylvia Klein, and French translation from the English by Anne-Laure Levain.

Altar Pieces, spiritual stories and lyrical poems written by Corinne Copnick. Originally produced by Janet Spiegel in 1992 as an innovative video called *Look at the Book!,* the stories were narrated by the author and the poems by actor Shelley Spiegel. It was licensed by *Vision TV*, Canada, in 1992, and screened for five years as a half-hour television show on its educational network. Artwork by acclaimed Canadian artist, the late Saul Field. ©Corinne Copnick, Toronto, 1992; Los Angeles, 2023. All rights reserved.

How To Live Alone Until You Like It...And Then You Are Ready For Somebody Else, was written when author Corinne Copnick was resident writer at the Banff Centre for the Arts in Alberta, where she was a guest of the Leighton Artists Colony. This book tells the story of a woman in her 50s, one who has lived most of her life in togetherness—with a husband, children, and large, extended family—learning to live apart as a single woman in a time of evolving feminism. Eventually she considers herself a survivor with a highly developed sense of humor. Cartoons by Don Merrifield. Published by La Magie de l'Art Inc., ©Corinne Copnick,

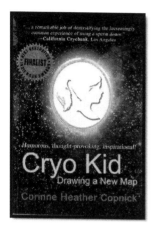

Cryo Kid: Drawing a New Map is an exploration, inspired by true experience, of her daughter's fertility journey at a time when artificial means of conception for single women were just emerging. Written with insightful humor and a sense of wonder from the perspective of a seventy-something grandmother, it is educational, positive, and eye-opening. The author, Corinne Heather Copnick (Grandma), explores the exponential transformation that has taken place in families in her lifetime, as well as the infertility crisis currently experienced by career women who waited too long to have children. Published by iUniverse, Inc., 2008.

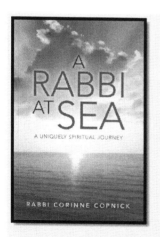

In *A Rabbi at Sea: A Uniquely Spiritual Journey*, Rabbi Copnick narrates the stories of her travel experiences as a guest rabbi on cruise ships. On every journey and in every country visited, she uncovered, discovered, and explored Jewish life—from Hawaii to Australia, the Mediterranean, North Africa, Southeast Asia, Central and South America, and everywhere in between. Offering a global perspective, she presents a host of insights about the culture and the people she encountered throughout her travel. *A Rabbi at Sea* shares Rabbi Copnick's anecdotal exploration of the tapestry of world Jewry in fascinating locales around the world. It offers a treasure trove of her reflections on history, spirituality, and humanity. Published by Lulu Press, Inc., Los Angeles, 2020.

NOTES

[1] ©Corinne Copnick, Toronto, 1989; Los Angeles, 2023. Adapted from *Altar Pieces*, video stories by Corinne Copnick, screened nationally on Vision TV, Canada, 1992-1997.

[2] The thoughts in this expanded version were first expressed in part in an article I wrote for the *Women's Alliance* (Naples, Florida) 2021 newsletter to initiate their new Writers' Group, ©Corinne Copnick, Los Angeles, 2023. All rights reserved.

[3] "The Middle of the Air," *Altar Pieces,* ©Corinne Copnick,1992. Toronto, Canada. All rights reserved..

[4] ©Corinne Copnick Spiegel, *Embrace:A Love Story in Poetry; Etreinte: Un poeme d'amour,* French trans. by Anne-Laure Levain (Montreal: Editions Guy Maheux, La Societe de Belle Lettres de Quebec, 1981; *Corinne Copnick*, Los Angeles, 2023), 53. Bilingual (English/French). All rights reserved. Out of print, rare book.

[5] Richard Siegel and Rabbi Laura Geller. *Getting Good at Getting Older* (Los Angeles: Behrman Books, 2019).

[6] Rabbi Bradley Shavit Artson, "A Secret Aging: How You Can Ward Off Death," *Jewish Journal*, Los Angeles, Sept. 13-19, 2019, 49. Rabbi Artson holds the Abner and Roslyn Goldstine Dean's chair of the Ziegler School of Rabbinic Studies at American Jewish University in Los Angeles. He has authored more than 200 books and articles.

[7] Moses was 80 and Aaron 81 when they confronted the Pharaoh in a complementary fashion.

[8] Artson, "*A Secret Aging.*" See also *Seder Nezkin, Pirkei Avot*, chapter 5. The *Pirkei Avot* is a compilation of the ethics, teachings, and maxims passed down from Moses onward. It seems as relevant to modern societies as it was when it was written.

[9] "Artson, (quoting Abraham Joshua Heschel in "To Grow in

Wisdom"), "Bearing Fruit in Old Age," *Judaism*, Spring Issue, 1977, *http://www.myjewishlearning.com,*

[10] Artson, *Jewish Journal*, Los Angeles, 49.

[11] *https://www.brainyquote.com,* accessed 2023.

[12] Hebrew for "Home for Everyone," or, as I prefer, "Home of Togetherness."

[13] Hebrew for "May you go from strength to strength."

[14] *https://www.salk.edu,* accessed 2023.

[15] When I was a young girl in Montreal during the polio epidemic, the polio vaccine had not yet been created, so I was never vaccinated against the disease. Fortunately, all four of my children were, and, of course, my grandchildren. I remember vividly how all the public swimming pools and libraries were closed, and that my mother wouldn't let me open letters from my pen-pal in Milwaukee, where the disease was raging.

[16] *https://www.brainyquote.com*, accessed 2023.

[17] This passage is included in my article, Corinne Copnick, "Interpersonal Ethics: Our Partner in Digital Citizenship." *Torah, Service, Deeds: Jewish Ethics in Transdenominational Perspectives*, ©2023 by the authors. All rights reserved. Ben Yehuda Press, 2023 (Tea Neck, N.J., 2023), p. 63.

[18] Micah 6: 8-12, *https://www.sefaria.org,* English translation from *JPS Hebrew-English Tanakh* (Philadelphia: Jewish Publication Society, 1985).

[19] Exodus 3:14, *https://www.sefaria.org*, English translation from *JPS Hebrew-English Tanakh* (Philadelphia: Jewish Publication Society, 1985).

[20] Rabbi Jonathan Sacks, "How The Jewish People Invented Hope," *My Jewish Learning, https://www.myjewishlearning.com/article/how-the-*

jewish-people-invented-hope.

23 In an online Q+A, Brian Greene spoke with key project scientists about the telescope's first full color images...providing unprecedented observations of the birth of stars and the formation of galaxies." This program is part of the "Big Ideas" series, supported by the John Templeton Foundation and televised on CNN (July, 2022).

22 Some articles suggested our understanding may change more than we currently know. See Nola Taylor, below.

23 "What is dark matter?" by Nola Taylor, posted on *Space.com*, Jan. 28, 2022.

24 CNN, "Big Ideas," televised Jan. 28, 2022.

25 Google, accessed December, 2022.

26 Interview with Ari Melber on "The Beat," CNN, August 24, 2022.

27 Google, accessed December, 2002.

28 According to an article in the *Jewish Journal* (Artson, "Almighty? No Way! Coming to Know the God We Already Love," Los Angeles, May 14-20, 2010, 22).

29 "Almighty, No Way," *Jewish Journal*. Apparently, process thought was "first articulated by mathematician/philosopher Alfred North Whitehead, enhanced by philosopher Charles Hartshore, and applied by theologian John Cobb."

30 "Almighty, No Way," *Jewish Journal*.

31 Rabbi Joshua Ladon, "Nostalgia, Narrative, and Renewal," L.A. Board of Rabbis High Holiday Workshop 2022 address, August 23, 2022.

32 See Goedele Baeke et al, "'There is a Time to be Born and a Time to Die' (Ecclesiastes 3:2a): Jewish Perspectives on Euthanasia," *Journal of Religion and Health* (January 2011) for an extended discussion

of this issue. See also *Bavli Ketubot* 104a, *Bavli Avodah Zureh* 18a; and *Bavli Ketubot* 104a, all found in the Talmud.

[33] Baeke et al., *Time to be Born*.

[34] Yogi Berra was a very famous baseball catcher. He was also valued for his pithy statements on life, which have endured beyond his baseball career.

[35] "Continuity," *Embrace*, 89.

[36] Carl Sagan, *The Pale Blue Dot*, 1990. Quoted in *CNN Morning Brew*, July 17, 2022.

[37] Sagan, *The Pale Blue Dot*.

[38] Abraham Joshua Heschel, *The Sabbath*, Farrar, Straus and Giroux, New York, 1951; ©renewed 1979 by Sylvia Heschel; Introduction ©2005 by Susanna Heschel. Paperback edition, 2005, 100.

[39] Jonathan Sacks, "Future Tense: How the Jews Invented Hope," *https://www.rabbisacks.org/archive*, April 1, 2008.

[40] Sacks, "Future Tense…", *https://www.rabbisacks.org/archive*, April 1, 2008.

[41] In the Tower of Babel story, human beings outraged God by trying to usurp God's power: They built a very tall tower in attempting to reach the heavens. God then punished humans by dispersing them to different locales and disrupting their communications by giving them different languages so they could not understand one another.

[42] "To A Mouse: On Turning Her Up in her Nest, With the Plough," November, 1785. For those who are not familiar with the poetry of Robert Burns, the term *"gang aft agley"* is the old Scottish way of poetically saying "often gone astray."

[43] See Jack Miles, *God: A Biography*. (Alfred A. Knopf, 1995; Vintage, 1996.)

---

[44] Included in my rabbinic thesis (2014) and retold in many of my subsequent talks.

[45] *Song of Songs Rabbah*, 1-24. Torah commentary on the Covenant/Brit by Rabbi Joseph Telushkin, *Jewish Literacy*, (William Morrow/Harper Collins, revised ed., 2008: New York) 40. Telushkin references his own source as Jeremiah Unterman, "Covenant," in Paul Achtemeir, ed., *Harper's Bible Dictionary*, 190-192.

[46]A very religious Orthodox Jew.

[47] Literally, a *mitzvah* refers to fulfilling a commandment, but is commonly referred to as doing "a good deed." In any case, it is a blessing to do either one—or both.

[48] In the Jewish tradition, the giving of the ten commandments at Mount Sinai was witnessed not only by those present, but by every Jewish person through the generations. The intent is to give immediacy to the commandments. In this mystical sense, both the young *Hasid* and I were present at Sinai.

[49]PEN was originally an acronym for Poets, Essayists, and Novelists, and writers had to be invited to belong. Today it is a huge and highly respected international organization that also includes Playwrights and diverse other writers.

[50] When I wrote this true story about an event my sister and I witnessed that took place one very cold Toronto night in 1992 and that, given the circumstances, seemed to be miraculous in nature, we had no idea in that jubilant atmosphere that what we most feared would transpire thirty years later in Chattauqua, New York

[51] Graham Gibson, then President of PEN Canada, and the husband of Margaret Atwood, and several other writers, like John Ralston Saul, are to be commended for inviting Rushdie and for the complex organization and security arrangements that followed.

[52] "Rushdie later described the evening as one 'he would never

forget'" (PEN Canada newsletter, 2012, celebrating the 20th anniversary of Rushdie's secret visit to Toronto).

[53] On August 13, 2022, three decades after the historic 1992 PEN reading in Toronto, a distinguished literary event took place in Chauttaqua, New York: The internationally acclaimed author, Salman Rushdie, knighted by the Queen of England, was talking about his latest book when a furious attacker, jumping onto the stage, stabbed Rushdie multiple times. The author, then 75, was rushed to the hospital, and the 24-year old assailant was quickly captured. According to media reports, Rushdie's liver was badly damaged; the nerves of one arm were severed; and he was in danger of losing one eye. As some reporters noted, after thirty years, the Fatwa had been fulfilled. Fortunately, Rushdie recovered sufficiently to begin the long process of healing. (*www.NYTimes.com*, Aug. 14, 2022; *www.washingtonpost.com,* Aug. 14, 2022; *www.CNN.com.* Aug. 14, 2022).

[54] This chapter is an adaptation of a core chapter in my rabbinic thesis.

[55] Isaiah 43:1-15, *https://www.sefaria.org,* English translation from *JPS Hebrew-English Tanakh* (Philadelphia: Jewish Publication Society, 1985).

[56] Irving Greenberg, "Faith, Hope, & Redemption," *The Living Pulpit,* (April-June, 1992), p. 12.

[57] Pirke Avot 1:7.

[58] Pirke Avot 1:7.

[59] See Sigmund Freud, *The Future of an Illusion*, trans. James Strachey (London: W.W. Norton and Co., 1927, German edition; 1928, 1989, English edition).

[60] Michael Marmur, "Lifeline to the Future," accessed May 5, 2013, *http://reformjudaism.org/Articles*, 3.

[61]Tal Becker, "How To Be An Optimist in the Middle East,"

accessed February 6, 2013, *http://www.hartman.org.il*, 1.

[62] Aviva Zornberg, *The Beginning of Desire: Reflections on Genesis* (New York: Schocken Books, 1995), 303.

[63] David Hartman, "Sinai and Exodus: Two Grounds for Hope in the Jewish Tradition," 147-52.

[64] Bradley Shavit Artson, "The Crack is How the Light Gets In," *Today's Torah*, Ziegler School of Rabbinic Studies, accessed September 2013.

[65] Over time, different concepts have modified and enriched the concept of redemption: In the Torah, redemption (*ge'ulah* in biblical Hebrew) concerns the ransom of slaves in primarily three categories: Israelite slave, Israelite captive, or first born son (Exodus 2:18). Later, in Rabbinic Judaism, redemption refers to God redeeming the Israelites (as God's firstborn), from their exiles, starting with the exile from Egypt and including redemption from the present exile and applies to both individuals and groups. In Hasidic philosophy, parallels are drawn between the redemption from exile and the personal redemption achieved when a person refines his/her character traits and does *teshuva*—repentance, restitution, and good deeds—to compensate for wrongs. Messianic redemption is linked to looking toward Mount Zion (toward Jerusalem), one of the religious and cultural associations of Zionism. Drawing inspiration from the priests and prophets as well as King David and King Cyrus in past times, the concept of redemption may involve the Messiah (*Moshiach*), the anointed and long-anticipated Jewish leader (who will be a fine human being descended from King David), and who will usher in an era of world peace and godly awareness. (See *https://en.wikipedia.org>wiki>Jewish-escatologhe* and various *Chabad* websites: *https://www.chabad.org*.)

[66] David Hartman. "Sinai and Exodus: Two Grounds for Hope in the Jewish Tradition," 374.

[67] *Sanhedrin 97 b*. The passage parallels the views of the Tannaitic teachers, R. Eliezer ben Hyrcanus and R. Yehoshua, both students of R. Johanan ben Zakkai.

[68] Sanhedrin 97b .

[69] Furthermore, Hartman explains the traditional view that, the Messiah will come in a generation when all are either meritorious or guilty (Babylonian Talmud, *Sanhedrin* 98a)

[70] Hartman, "Sinai and Exodus: Two Grounds for Hope in the Jewish Tradition," 378.

[71] Hartman, "Sinai and Exodus: Two Grounds for Hope in the Jewish Tradition," 373.

[72] This chapter is an adaptation of material that originally appeared in my rabbinic thesis.

[73] Eugene B. Borowitz, "Hope Jewish and Hope Secular," *Judaism*, New York, Vol. 17, Iss.2, (Spring 1968). A controversial study by the Pew Research Foundation supports Borowitz' claims about increased Jewish secularization.

[74] Zornberg, *The Beginning of Desire*, 301-303.

[75] Thus, in exploring what she calls "the dialectical tension" between the twin Hebrew words of *shever* and *sever*, she explains that, in Hebrew, hope [*sever*, an approximate synonym for *tikvah*] is contained within the word for brokenness [*shever*].

[76] Zornberg, *The Beginning of Desire*, 301.

[77] Zornberg, *The Beginning of Desire*, 302.

[78] ©Corinne Copnick Spiegel, Montreal, 1978; 1981; Los Angeles, 2023. My poem was first selected for the anthology, *There Is A Voice*, A Collection of English Poetry and Photography by Montreal Women, Ed. Wendy Wachtel (Montreal, Canada: Angle Lightning Press, 1978) 27. I subsequently included it in my first book of bilingual poems, *Embrace/Etreinte* (Montreal: Edition Guy Maheux, 1981) 21.

[79] See Harold Kushner, *When Bad Things Happen to Good People*

(New York:: Schocken Books, 1984).

[80] Zornberg, *The Beginning of Desire,* 303.

[81] David R. Blumenthal, "Despair and Hope in Post-Shoah Jewish Life," *Bridges, 6:3, 4* (1999): 128.

[82] Blumenthal, "Despair and Hope in Post-Shoah Jewish Life," 128

[83] Elie Wiesel, "Hope, Despair, and Memory," *Modern American Poetry,* Nobel Lecture, accessed Dec. 11, 1986, *https://www.nobelprize.org/prizes/peace/1986/wiesel/lecture/*, 4.

[84] Wiesel, "Hope, Despair and Memory."

[85] Archibald MacLeish's famous but rather depressing play about Job, *J. B.* (Boston: Houghton Mifflin, 1958), ends by presenting hope as the only solution to continuing life that has suffered the catastrophe. Also See Dr. Jacob Zighelboim. *From Fear to Awe: A New Understanding of the Book of Job Brings the Sufferer to Wholeness* (Los Angeles: Toren Publishers, 1986).

[86]Frankl survived four Nazi death camps, including Auschwitz, but lost most family members in World War II. Yet through his famous book, *Man's Search for Meaning* (Mass.: Beacon Press, 2006) and his counseling work ("logotherapy,") he taught others about spiritual survival by finding personal meaning (from the Greek word, *logos*) in suffering and new purpose in moving forward. He died in 1997.

[87] From back cover of *Man's Search for Meaning,* which sold ten million copies. (Mass.: Beacon Press, 2006)

[88] *https://jewishaction.com,* "Responsa from the Holocaust," (accessed March 31, 2014).

[89] *Mishna Torah,* Bk. 1., Ch. 10:6. In Isadore Twersky, ed. *A Maimonides Reader,* 85.

[90] "Rabbi Oshry wrote the questions and answers about Jewish

law on scraps of paper... placed these notes in tin cans, and buried them.... After the liberation of Kovno in August, 1944, Rabbi Oshry retrieved the hidden archive and published five volumes of responsa." *https://jewishaction.com,* "Responsa from the Holocaust," (accessed March 31, 2014).

91 *Teshuva* refers to Repentance. For complete repentance, you must first make restitution to the injured party or parties, and then sufficiently repent so that when a similar circumstance occurs, you act differently. I wrote this story in Hannah's memory after she had passed away.

92 *www.rabbiwein.com/Kuzari.*

93 Corinne Copnick, *Altar Pieces.*

94 *https://en.wikipedia.org/wiki/Soviet_Jewry.*

95 *https://en.wikipedia.org/wiki/Soviet_Jewry.*

96 *https://en.wikipedia.org/wiki/Soviet_Jewry.*

97 Today human rights activist, Natan Sharansky, is an Israeli politician and author, whose opinions are esteemed in the Western world. During the Cold War, he was known widely as a Soviet refusnik, imprisoned for his oppositional stands.

98 His memoir of those years, *Fear No Evil,* was translated into nine languages. Subsequent books that he wrote, *The Case for Democracy: The Power of Freedom to Overcome Tyranny and Terror* (2004) were influential in high places. His latest book (with Shira Wolosky) is *Defending Identity: Its Indispensable Role in Protecting* Democracy (New York: Public Affairs, Perseus Books, 2004). (*https://www.jewishvirtuallibrary.org*).

99 Dr. Joel Gereboff, email, June, 2013.

100 Oppenheim, Michael, "Irving Greenberg and a Jewish Dialectic of Hope." *Judaism: A Quarterly Journal of Jewish Life and Thought,* 49:2 (2000): 189-203. He is also the author of *Speaking/Writing of God: Jewish*

Philosophical Reflections on Life with Others (1997).

[101] Oppenheim, "Irving Greenberg," 197.

[102] Oppenheim, "Irving Greenberg," 197.

[103] Oppenheim, "Irving Greenberg," 198.

[104] Eugene B. Borowitz, "Hope Jewish and Hope Secular," 131-147.

[105] Borowitz, "Hope Jewish and Hope Secular," 144.

[106] Dara Horn, *People Love Dead Jews: Reports from a Haunted Present*, Kindle Edition, 2021. In 2021, winner of the National Book Award for Contemporary Jewish Life and Practice; NYT Notable Book of the Year; Wall Street Journal; Chicago Public Library; Publishers Weekly; and Kirkus Best Books of the Year.

[107] Corinne Copnick Spiegel, *Embrace*, 83.

[108] Identified by Jeffrey L. Rubenstein. *Talmudic Stories: Narrative Art, Composition and Culture* (Baltimore, Maryland: John Hopkins Press, 1999). Also, *Context and Genre: Elements of a Literary Approach to the Rabbinic Narrative* in *How Should Rabbinic Literature Be Read In The Modern World?*, ed. Matthew Kraus (N.J.: Georgia Press, 2006).

[109] Burton L. Vizotsky, *Sage Tales*: Wisdom and Wonder from the Rabbis of the Talmud (USA: Jewish Lights, 2011), 14, 187.

[110] Rabbi Elijah J. Schochet, who taught me to love the many perspectives and enduring wisdom of the Talmud. Lecture, AJRCA, 2012.

[111] The feminine aspect of God.

[112] ©Corinne Copnick, *Cryo Kid: Drawing a New Map*, 2008, 150. This poem was originally published in the August, 1990 newsletter of the Banff Arts Center, Alberta (where I was honored to be a Resident Writer at the Leighton Artist Colony.) The poem reflected my feelings about that still-treasured, other-worldly experience, one of the best gifts anyone

ever gave me.

[113] *Major Noah: American Zionist, Mordecai Manuel Noah,* *http://www.jewish-american-society-for-historic-preservation.org/*

[114] *http://www.jewishvirtuallibrary.org.* Mount Arafat was believed by some Jews to be the place where Noah's Ark landed. To date, the claim has not been substantiated.

[115] Jonathan D. Sarna, Ph.D. *Jacksonian Jew: The Two Worlds of Mordecai Noah.* Dr. Sarna is also Chief Historian of the National Museum of American Jewish History in Philadelphia.

[116]Exodus 6:6-8, *https://www.sefaria.org*, English translation from *JPS Hebrew-English Tanakh* (Philadelphia: Jewish Publication Society, 1985).

[117] In comparison to the eight miles by six miles dimensions of Grand Island, the island of Montreal is 31 miles long and 9.9 miles wide at its widest point.

[118] Deut. 34:1-5, *https://www.sefaria.orkh*, English translation from *JPS Hebrew-English Tanakh* (Philadelphia: Jewish Publication Society, 1985).

[119] Published in 1895. His next book, *Alt Neu'land,* a novel, was published in 1902 and presented the new land as potentially enriching for both Jews and Arabs.

[120] Psalm 137: 5-6, English trans., *https://www.Safaria.org*.

[121] *Pirkei Avot*, 2:21

[122] Corinne Copnick, *Altar Pieces.*

[123] Eugene B. Borowitz, "Hope Jewish and Hope Secular": 131-147. In earlier times, there was lots of discussion about hope, he says, particularly in regard to Israel, but the sources tended to be biblical, not Talmudic.

---

[124] Borowitz, "Hope Jewish and Hope Secular", 138.

[125] Greenberg, "Faith, Hope, and Redemption," 12a.

[126] Blumenthal, "Despair and Hope in Post-Shoah Jewish Life," 129.

[127] Originally published as "Transplantation" in *Altar Pieces*, ©Corinne Copnick, Toronto, 1992. All rights reserved.

[128] ©Corinne Copnick, Los Angeles, 2017. All rights reserved. I never read this poem to my sister; I wrote it after she had passed away.

[129] See Sandra Caplan Community Bet Din, *www.exec scbetdin. us.com.*

[130] American Jewish Committee, *Translate Hate: Stopping Antisemitism Starts with Understanding It,* Oct. 2021, accessed Sept. 6, 2022.

[131] The Zionist movement has been falsely associated by anti-Jewish propagandists with racism; hence the *Zionism is racism* meme. Antisemitic political pressure eventually led to the United Nations Resolution 3379 in 1975, "in which the General Assembly linked Zionism and the State of Israel to racism and racial discrimination. This was overturned in 1991, making it one of only two resolutions ever revoked by the UN." (American Jewish Committee, *Translate Hate*, October, 2021). In *Translate Hate*, available online, the distinguished American Jewish Committee describes Zionism (until 1948, a long-held aspiration) as a reality today.

[132] Originally, *Hatikvah*, then called *"Tikvatenu,"* meaning "Our Hope," was composed ca. 1876 or 1877 by Naftali Herz Iber as a nine-stanza poem. In 1933 it became the anthem of the 18th Zionist Congress. Then, when the State of Israel became a reality, the first stanza and refrain were adopted as the State of Israel's national anthem. There is some opposition to the Anthem among different groups (mainly among very Orthodox Israelis because there are no references to God in it, and

from some pro-Palestinian enemies of Israel, who—ignoring the warrior emphasis of their own anthem—consider it racist). Alternate anthems were written but did not take hold. Despite the controversy, most Jewish people both in and out of Israel, love *Hatikvah* and it remains the national anthem of Israel. The melody is accredited to Samuel Cohen, although its roots may be traced to a 16th century Italian song. Born in Moldavia-Romania, Samuel Cohen settled in Rishon LeZion during the First Aliyah (*https://jr.co.il/hatikva.htm*; also see Knesset Website.)

[133] *https://jr.co.il/hatikva.ht*

[134] *https://jr.co.il/hatikva.ht*

[135]"Do Jews Really Believe in Miracles," *www.My Jewish Learning.com*, 1, accessed 5/4/2021.

[136]Reprinted from *How to Live Alone Until You Like It...and Then You Are Ready for Somebody Else* (©Corinne Copnick, La Magie de l'Art : Toronto, 1994; Los Angeles, 2023) 242-245.

[137] Corinne Copnick, *How To Live Alone,* 245-246.

[138] A *shoichet* is a ritual slaughterer who kills animals humanely. I first narrated this story to a large assemblage of Jewish performing artists and writers in Toronto and have told it many times since.

[139] *Great Jewish Thinkers of the Twentieth Century,* ed. Simon Noveck (USA: B'nai Brith Department of Adult Jewish Education, 1963), 190.

[140] Maurice Lamm, *The Power of Hope: The One Essential of Life and Love* (New York: Fireside, 1997), 143.

[141] Hartman, "Sinai and Exodus: Two Grounds for Hope in the Jewish Tradition," 387.

[142] David J. Wolpe, "My Last Cancer Treatment," Healthy Living, *Huffington Post, http://www.huffingtonpost.com/rabbi-david-wolpe/my-last-cancer-treatment_b_182379.html*, 1, accessed April 2, 2009.

---

143 David J. Wolpe, "My Last Cancer Treatment," 1

144 Naomi Levy, *Hope Will Find You: My Search for the Wisdom to Stop Waiting and Start Living* (New York: Harmony Books, Sept 21, 2010), 22.

145 Levy, *Hope Will Find You* , 152.

146The story of Nachshon is told in both the Midrash and the Talmud (*Mechilta, Beshalach* 5; *Pirkei d'Rabbi Eliezer* 42; *Exodus Rabbah* 13; and others, as well as *Sotah* 37A. He was given this name, Nachson, because he courageously jumped into the waves (*nachshol*) of the sea, encouraging the Israelites to save themselves from the Egyptians by following his lead (Mindy Kaminker, "*Nachshon ben Aminadav*: The Man who Jumped into the Sea.," *https://www.chabad.org/library article_cdp/zid/2199147*. Accessed 1/6/22, p.1.)

147 *http://www.sefaria.org/, Bava Metzia, Ch. 2-3*

148 This story was included in my rabbinic thesis and previously appeared in *Altar Pieces* (1992). I have included it in my talks many times.

149 Others lost all hope. Most who lost hope did not survive, or, if they did, they often emerged from this horrible experience with great bitterness. Compare Primo Levi's dark recollections, for example, in his landmark book, *Survival in Auschwitz* (originally published as *If This Is A Man*), which described his year as a prisoner in Auschwitz in Nazi-occupied Poland.

150 A recent article by Rabbis Michael J. Broyde and Michael Hecht explained this aspect of Jewish law: "The Return of Lost Property According to Jewish and Common Law: A Comparison," *Jewish Law Articles: Examining Halacha, Jewish Issues and Secular Law*, accessed 3/15/2011, *http://www.jlaw.com/Articles.*

151 For these reasons, I included it in my rabbinic thesis, and now it is here for your enjoyment. But it wasn't so funny when it happened to me!

[152]Authors Brodye and Hecht ("The Return of Lost Property") claim that Jewish law and U.S. common law regarding lost property coincide. However, in areas where common law is hazy, Jewish law is more detailed:

"Jewish law recognizes that property may become ownerless by one of two means:

1) abandonment, which is an express renunciation by the former owner of his ownership; or 2) express or implied "forsaking hope" of reclaiming an object to which one has legal title, but not possession by the owner of that item. Abandonment is effective only for property in one's own possession at the time of abandonment. By contrast, forsaking hope is applicable to both lost and stolen property; it is a relinquishment of the right to have the property returned. It results from external, involuntary circumstances which have placed the property beyond the possession of the owner, and the owner's realization that he is unlikely to ever recover his property," (*http://www.jlaw.com/Articles*, accessed 3/15, 2011).

[153]©Corinne Copnick, Toronto, 1994; Los Angeles, 2014. This story first appeared as part of *Altar Pieces*, a videotaped narration of Rabbi Copnick's stories and poems that was screened nationally many times on Canada's Vision TV over a period of five years. "The Boy" is a fictionalized account inspired by a true Bar Mitzvah ritual at which the author was present.

[154] This poem was written by my late father, Dr. Irving Copnick, when he served as a Captain in the Canadian Army, attached to the British Airforce during World War II. He was stationed in London, England but hospitalized there after his mobile ambulance with a big red cross on the roof was strafed from the air by German planes. During the blitz, the dentists helped doctors to identify people who had been killed through comparison of their teeth with dental records. They also assisted in repairing shattered jaws. His poem, which he titled "Tooth-Ache," was published in several military newsletters. He died in 1992. I wrote my group of filmed stories, *Altar Pieces,* in his honor.

[155] The letters z"l are a Hebrew abbreviation of *Zichrono livracha* meaning "of blessed memory."

---

[156] This story appeared in *Altar Pieces*.

[157] Not long after my father's death, I saw a feature film called *Awakening*, which told the story of a man with sleeping sickness who awoke from his coma of many years. He recounted that, although unable to make a sign of any kind, he had heard everything spoken in his hearing while imprisoned in his body. Unfortunately, after a little time, the sleeping sickness reclaimed him. This is an important film for rabbis to see. At this writing, it is still available on one of the Internet sites or on DVD.

[158] A.J. Seltzer, "Beyond the Right to Die, Will it Become a Duty to Die?" *Human Aging: The Journey of Soul Return* (2001), 1.

[159] *https://www.sefaria.org*

[160] Baeke et al, There is a Time to be Born, 2000.

[161] Baeke et al, *There is a Time to be Born*, 2000. See Jokobovits, 1959, p. 121; Sinclair, p.9; Sinclair 2003, p. 181; *Semachot* 1:1-4.

[162] Baeke et al, *There is a time to be Born*, 2000, 313. Cited by Rabbi Eliot Dorff, a Conservative Rabbi.

[163] Should the physician make the decision? If not, who makes the decision? Do you listen to the dying person of the relatives? The insurance company and what it will "cover"? Should the patient be accorded heroic treatment if death is imminent? Will the relatives have peace of mind that they did everything they could? How does one take into account a living will that needs to be updated or advance directives? When situations like these come up, it can be very helpful to consult a rabbinic authority for spiritual direction.

[164] Arthur D. Silk,"Beyond the Right to Die, Will it Become a Duty to Die? *Human Aging: The Journey of Soul Return* (2001), 1

[165] Excerpt from Ernest Raab, *Violin of Stone,* trans. Jeremy Fox, ed. Corinne Copnick (Toronto: Lugus Publishing, 1999), 140-141. The author, my good friend when I lived in Toronto, passed away several years

ago, and, to date, I have been unable to contact the book's publisher nor any member of Raab's family.

¹⁶⁶ While Raab was still a teenager interned in a work camp during World War II, his entire village and family that had remained in Hungary were blown up by explosions. This is his moving testimony (written twenty years later in French) of when he heard the news. Ironically, the explosion was caused by Allied bombers who blew up a munitions factory in the town in the last months of the war. After the war, Raab became a famous sculptor in Canada, creating a huge Holocaust memorial in Toronto and many other magnificent commissions for synagogues in that city and elsewhere.

¹⁶⁷Ernest Raab's Hebrew name.

¹⁶⁸ Ernest Raab, *Violin of Stone,* 140-141.

¹⁶⁹ "We recite the *Sh'ma* to bear witness to the Oneness of God." *Mishkan T'filah: A Reform Siddur.* Central Conference of American Rabbis, New York, 2007 (5767), 10.

¹⁷⁰"These words are to be said immediately upon waking from sleep. In them we thank God for life itself, renewed each day. Sleep, said the Sages, is 'one-sixtieth of death' (*Yerushalmi, Berakhot* 1a). Waking, therefore, is a miniature rebirth. *The Koren Siddur, Intro, trans. and commentary by the late Rabbi Sir Jonathan Sacks*: First Hebrew/English Edition (Koren Publishers, Jerusalem, 2009) 5.

¹⁷¹ Jon D. Levenson, *Resurrection and the Restoration of Israel: The Ultimate Victory of the God of Life* (Chelsea, Michegan: Sheridan Books, Yale University, 2006), 131.

¹⁷² Conversation with Rabbi David Woznica, Zeldin Chair, Stephen Wise Temple, Los Angeles, Autumn, 2022.

¹⁷³ Just as the banana trees I once saw on a St. Lucia plantation gracefully descend to join the earth in synchronicity with the young banana shoots ascending slowly from their parent-trees' roots toward the sky. Nature offers some inspiring lessons.

---

[174] The study of Epigenetics concerns how both behaviors and environment may cause changes to the way our genes work. These are heritable and reversible changes that do not alter DNA sequence. However, they may affect the way the body reads a DNA sequence.

[175] Bruce H. Lipton, Ph.D., *The Biology of Belief: Unleashing the Power of Consciousness, Matter, and Miracles,* 10th Anniversary edition. (Australia, India, U.K., U.S., CA: Hay House of Publishers, 2023), 209. (©2005 by Bruce Lipton; Revised ©2008; Updated 2015; Reprint 2023. I originally read the 2005 version and recently re-read the 2023 reprint.)

[176] Lipton, *The Biology of Belief,* 209.

[177] Lipton, *The Biology of Belief* 209.

[178] Lipton, *The Biology of Belief*, Prologue, pp. xv-xvi.

[179] Rabbi Jonathan Sacks, *The Dignity of Difference: How To Avoid the Clash of Civilizations.*(London: Continuum, 2003), 2007. Also available on multiple internet sites, such as Scribd or Brill.com, as a downloadable pdf. (© attribution is non-commercial.)

[180] https://www.sefaria.org

[181] Rabbi Yonatan Neril and Rabbi Leo Dee, co-editors and lead contributors, *Eco Bible, vol. 1: An Ecological Commentary on Genesis and Exodus*, The Interfaith Center for Sustainable Development (www.interfaithsustain.com), XX.

[182] Neril and Dee, *Eco Bible*, 191.

[183] Midrash, *Kohelet Rabbah* (*Ecclesiastes Rabbah*), *https://www.sefaria.org*

[184] Deut. 20:19, *https://www.sefaria.org*

[185] First published in my book, *Cryo Kid: Drawing a New Map,* 2008, 149-150. I originally wrote this poem in Banff, Alberta in the summer of 1990, when, in the midst of magnificent mountains and an

abundance of breathtaking scenery, I came upon a newspaper stand displaying ugly headlines about increasingly possible war—once again. At the time, I was spending a blissful summer as a Resident Writer at the renowned Leighton Artist Colony, Banff Centre for the Arts, Alberta, in Canada.

[186] Levy, *Hope Will Find You*, 70.

[187] Reported in a lead article by Science reporter for the *New York Times*, Kenneth Chung, December 13, 2022, "Scientists Achieve Nuclear Fusion Breakthrough With Blast of 192 Lasers," *https://www.nytimes.oseocom>72022/12/13 >science >nuclear-fusion-energy-breakthrough.html.*

[188] Chung, "Scientists Achieve Nuclear Fusion Breakthrough," Dec 13, 2022

[189] Chung, "Scientists Achieve Nuclear Fusion Breakthrough,"Dec 13, 2022

[190] Job 14:7-9,

[191] *https://www.nytimes.com <astronomy-webb-leda2046648.*

[192] They are *Embrace: A Love Story in Poetry (Etreinte: Une Poeme d'Amour)*, a bilingual book; *Altar Pieces; Metamorphose 77* (acclaimed play about drug abuse prevention, with cast of addicts in treatment); *How To Live Alone Until You Like It...And Then You're Ready For Somebody Else; Middle of the Air; Cryo Kid: Drawing a New Map; A Rabbi at Sea: An Uniquely Spiritual Journey*; and now *Miracles Are What You Make of Them*.

[193] I printed out the entire conversation (about 20 pages), which included the Chatbot professing its love for the human "chatting" with it when the transcript became available on the Internet. An historic moment!

[194] A Jewish folk legend tells the story of the *Maharal* of Prague, a learned rabbi wise in the ways of mysticism, who created a huge *golem*

out of clay in the attic of his house. The *golem* was intended to protect the persecuted Jews of Prague. But the mystical experiment did not end well. The first part of Michael Chabon's masterful novel , *Kavalier and Clay* describes the creation of this fictional super-hero of Prague for a 21st century literary audience.

195 ©Rachel Spiegel-Brown and Corinne Copnick, Los Angeles, 2023. All rights reserved.

196Babylonian Talmud (*Taanit* 19a; 23a), English Translation, *https://www.Sefaria.org* relates an often-told story about Honi and the Carob tree. The lesson that is taken away from this story is that if you give something you will not be alive to see, you are still giving."

197 The declaration was signed in Tel Aviv on the fifth day of Iyar, 5708 (May 14, 1948). The next day, as is well known, five Arab armies attacked the newly established State of Israel. They did not succeed.

Made in the USA
Columbia, SC
18 August 2023

21722717R00154